Workforce Development Networks in Rural Areas

Workforce Development Networks in Rural Areas

Building the High Road

Gary Paul Green

University of Wisconsin, Madison, USA

Edward Elgar

Cheltenham, UK • Northampton, MA, USA

Published by
Edward Elgar Publishing Limited
Glensanda House
Montpellier Parade
Cheltenham
Glos GL50 1UA
UK

Edward Elgar Publishing, Inc.
William Pratt House
9 Dewey Court
Northampton
Massachusetts 01060
USA

A catalogue record for this book
is available from the British Library

Library of Congress Cataloging in Publication Data

Green, Gary P.
    Workforce development networks in rural areas : building the high road / Gary Paul Green.
        p. cm.
    Includes bibliographical references and index.
    1. Rural development—United States. 2. Occupational training—United States. 3. Social networks—United States. I. Title
    HN90.C6G7245   2007
    331.12′042—dc22   2006016768

ISBN: 978 1 84542 872 3

Printed and bound MPG Books Ltd, Bodmin, Cornwall

Contents

Figures

List of tables

Acknowledgments

Several people have made major contributions to this project. Anna Haines was a key collaborator on much of the research project. Valeria Galetto conducted much of the fieldwork and is a coauthor on Chapter 5. Valeria was an incredible resource and conducted many of the interviews in Spanish and translated them for me. She has a knack for asking tough questions and digging for answers.

Christopher Mayhew helped with much of the data analysis and data preparation. John Stevenson, with the University of Wisconsin Survey Center provided important support with the design and implementation of the surveys.

I was fortunate enough to have Michael Dougherty work with me on the last eight months of this project. Michael was a spectacular research assistant and could find just the fact or figure I needed.

This material is based upon work supported by the Cooperative State Research, Education and Extension Service, US Department of Agriculture, National Research Initiative, under agreement no. 00-35401-9319. Any opinion, finding, conclusions, or recommendations expressed in this publication are those of the authors and do not necessarily reflect the view of the US Department of Agriculture. This work was also supported by the Agricultural Experiment Station (Hatch Project Number WIS04888) and the Institute for Research on Poverty at the University of Wisconsin-Madison.

I want to thank all of the organizations and institutions that participated in the study. The employers and community colleges were very considerate in their willingness to participate in our surveys. The community-based organizations were eager to help and were genuinely interested in our research and in finding ways to use this information.

I have thoroughly enjoyed working with Edward Elgar Publishing on this project. My editor, Tara Gorvine, was enthusiastic and supportive throughout the process. It is wonderful to be associated with such an excellent organization.

Finally, I want to thank my wife, Leann Tigges, and my daughter, Isabelle, for all of their support over the years. Much of what I have learned about local labor markets, I have gleaned from Leann's research and our discussions about work in rural areas. Many of her ideas are embedded in what follows. Isabelle continually reminds me about priorities and what really is important.

Gary Paul Green
Madison, WI

1. Introduction

Rural life has changed dramatically over the past century.[1] One of the most salient features of rural areas in the past was social isolation. Advances in telecommunications and transportation have integrated most rural communities into the larger society. Rural residents now have access to the internet, which allows them to shop and communicate with others outside their local community. Many rural workers commute to urban areas. Improvements in telecommunications also permit some people even to work at home, often relatively long distances from the business site in urban settings. Mass communications also provide rural residents with the same news and information that once was available only in the largest cities. They are therefore exposed to the same elements of mass culture that influence urbanites.

There also has been a transformation in how people earn a living in rural areas. Farming is no longer the primary occupation in most rural areas. Even in agricultural dependent areas, farming provides less income than other sources. Other extractive industries, like mining and forestry, no longer provide many jobs either. Technological change has been the major force displacing jobs in extractive industries. Today, the majority of workers in rural areas are now employed in the services sector.

This is not to suggest that rural–urban differences do not remain. Rural residents continue to maintain stronger ties and relationships with their neighbors than do urban residents. Similarly, rural residents tend to be more traditional and conservative with respect to their values and attitudes. Rural areas also tend to have less access to health and social services, primarily a result of the low population density in many rural communities.

One of the most persistent differences between rural and urban areas is the gap in wages and earnings. On average, rural workers in the US earn about 65 percent of the wages urban workers receive, and the difference is growing. Some of the income gap can be attributed to supply-side (human capital) factors, such as education, training and work experience. Rural workers have lower levels of formal education for several reasons. Rural areas attract older people who are likely to have less formal education. Younger residents are more likely to migrate to urban areas where they can obtain a college degree and increase their likelihood for advancement. Employers in rural areas are also less likely than urban employers to invest in job training for their workers. Historically, many rural areas also have suffered from labor shortages. Migrant workers, who tend to have lower levels of formal education and training, have been used to supplement the existing workforce in agricultural production and other extractive industries, and increasingly in the manufacturing sector in rural areas.

Differences in the demand for labor in rural and urban areas also contribute to the earnings gap. The industrial and occupational structures of rural and urban areas continue to differ in some important ways. Many of the economic problems facing rural regions are rooted in their dependency on industries that have experienced downward pressure on prices, technological change that has reduced the demand for workers, and oversupply due to international competition. Some of the best examples of these industries are agricultural and forest products industries, which have undergone rapid technological advances and increased international competition, especially since the 1970s. The manufacturing sector also has declined in many rural regions because firms have sought areas with even lower labor costs. Many of the manufacturing firms relocating to rural areas demand fewer skills and less training. Since the 1980s, services have contributed all the net new jobs in rural areas even though many of these jobs paid low wages and were part time (Glasmeier and Howland 1995). Despite the growth of services in rural communities, they have not necessarily produced a more stable economic economy. Consumer services are not considered an export industry and rely on other basic sectors of the economy. Producer services, which tend to pay higher wages, are more likely to be located in urban areas. Overall, the types of jobs and industries located in rural areas require less-skilled workers and tend to pay less than the jobs and industries in urban areas.

Demand for labor in rural areas is also shaped by the small population size and low density of these markets. These qualities make for 'thin' labor markets. By thin, I mean that the demand for various types of jobs is relatively small. Labor economists rarely look at the size of demand in local labor markets. Thin demand in rural labor markets may have several important effects, including the returns on investments in human capital and the rate of productivity growth. It also may contribute to problems in developing training programs for workers because there is not a sufficient critical mass of most skilled positions. As a result, rural labor markets tend to suffer from both a lack of skilled workers and paths of career mobility. Also, it usually means employers need to recruit for skilled workers outside the community. Because there are fewer employers competing for skilled workers, wages tend to be lower as well.

Differences in the institutional structure of rural and urban labor markets also may play a role in the earnings gap. Rural areas have fewer intermediaries (such as unions, community-based organizations and other institutions) that link workers to employers. Intermediaries provide information, training and, in some cases, assist in child care, transportation and housing. Without these intermediaries, it is difficult for rural labor markets to operate efficiently. Intermediaries help both workers and employers overcome the problems of lack of information that often plagues labor markets.

Some economists have argued that the wage gap between rural and urban workers simply reflects the preferences rural workers have for other elements of quality of life (Blanchflower and Oswald 1996). In other words, it is assumed that rural workers are willing to take lower wages in return for small town living, proximity to family and friends or access to natural resources and recreation. This argument, however, rests on several assumptions, such as workers are mobile and residence reflects rational choices of actors. Rural residents may not be as mobile as economists assume. Workers may have strong social ties that they may rely on in emergencies. To sacrifice this safety net is an extremely risky venture.

Residential preferences and location are, I think, endogenous. That is, there are reciprocal relationships between the two. There is not much empirical support for this claim that residential preferences determine where one lives. Rural workers are likely to say they prefer living in rural communities and urban workers are probably more likely to report that they like living in cities. This relationship between residential preferences and location can be due to a variety of conditions, especially lack of information and rationalizations about why they live where they do.

This argument about wages and residential preferences also ignores issues related to economic and social justice. Should rural workers who have the same level of training and education, and have essentially the same jobs as urban workers, earn less than urban workers? Urban workers also may be selectively mobile and are choosing to live in areas where they also receive quality of life benefits. They are not forced to make the same tradeoff that rural workers are. This issue regarding the role of residential preferences on earnings needs more attention, but at this point it raises more questions than answers about the earnings gap between rural and urban areas.

Overall, this discussion suggests that rural communities are faced with a dilemma in their efforts to promote economic development. If they invest more in formal education and training, there is a high probability that many workers will migrate to urban areas because of the lack of job opportunities. Rural communities are therefore incurring much of the cost of educating a workforce that largely will be employed in urban areas. Although they are generating a public good, rural communities may get very little return on these investments. In many regions, educational costs are borne largely by land owners and they may be more inclined to reduce expenditures for education if they do not see any local return on these investments.

On the other side of the equation, if rural communities are successful in attracting employers, there may not be a sufficient number of workers with the necessary skills for the jobs. In such cases, skilled workers may be imported from other regions. Although this may have some beneficial economic and fiscal impact on the region, it has few benefits for local workers who are seeking advancement. Some early work by Gene Summers *et al.* (1976) on rural industrialization found that as much as 80 to 90 percent of the workforce in branch plants locating in rural areas migrates for these jobs. Rural industrialization had little effect on the unemployment or poverty rate in rural areas. Thus, attracting new industry may not contribute as much to the regional economy because there are few opportunities for local residents. When tax incentives and subsidies are considered, there may be a net loss to the community.

An alternative economic development strategy is to create institutions that simultaneously build both the supply- and demand-side of rural labor markets. Historically rural areas have been the beneficiaries of the movement of capital to low cost areas. In recent years, however, this movement may have reached its limit due to the effects of globalization. New institutional arrangements are needed to help build the human capital of rural workers while helping employers make the transition to the new economy. Below, I discuss some of the issues rural areas face in this new era.

BUILDING THE HIGH ROAD

Although employers can adopt a variety of competitive strategies, some analysts have characterized the fundamental choice as between the 'high road' and the 'low road.' The low road involves competing against other firms in their industries by cutting production expenses, especially labor costs. Employers typically achieve this goal in several ways, such as moving to lower cost areas, outsourcing, or reducing training expenses. This strategy generates low rates of productivity growth and narrow profit margins. Adopting the low road approach, however, means that employers will have to compete directly against employers in other low cost areas. For example, much of the US textile industry has moved to China since 1990 as employers have been forced to move to even lower cost areas.

The high road strategy emphasizes technological adoption, investments in worker training and improvements in productivity. There are several different models for promoting the high road strategy. One of the influential books on this topic is Michael Piore and Charles Sabel's *The Second Industrial Divide* (1984). Piore and Sabel argue that successful economic regions, such as northern Italy, have made a transition from reliance on mass production to an economic system based on flexible specialization. Flexible specialization depends on permanent innovation, a highly skilled workforce and multiple use equipment (Piore and Sabel 1984: 17). Clusters of manufacturing firms in northwestern Italy are the exemplars for this model. Flexible specialization is the polar opposite of the mass production system, which is an institutional system that relies on mass markets, unskilled workers and standardization. Flexible specialization necessarily requires a high level of employer provided training to satisfy the technological requirements of the jobs. Because there are many employers in the region who have the same training needs, they can cooperate and coordinate their efforts.

Although policy-makers and scholars have been optimistic about the potential of high road systems such as flexible production, these models are not widely distributed across rural areas. Similarly, recently there has been a great deal of attention given to the 'creative' or 'knowledge' economy. Proponents of these ideas suggest that the path for economic development in rural regions should be based on increasing the number of high skilled jobs that are based on producing ideas rather than things. Yet, most of the analyses fail to provide a map of how rural communities can build a knowledge economy or how to overcome many of the structural and institutional obstacles rural communities face.

Why do most rural employers continue down the low road? What obstacles do they face in making the transition to the high road? We lack adequate answers to these questions. The availability and cost of credit can be an obstacle in many rural areas. New technology is expensive and the low profit rate of many firms does not generate enough capital for these investments. Access to debt capital can be a real problem in many rural areas and it may be difficult for employers to obtain loans in urban areas.

The real obstacle, I believe, is institutional. Educational and training institutions in rural areas offer a much more limited curriculum and often lack resources. Most rural areas do not have colleges or universities, which are frequently the spark for the growth of the knowledge economy. Nor do they have the cultural amenities and diversity that Richard Florida (2002) says contribute to the formation of a creative class. And as I will discuss in the next chapter, many rural areas suffer from a brain drain that makes it difficult to build the human capital that will support a knowledge economy.

The preferred solution is for employers to become more engaged in training their existing workforce (Streeck 1989). I will review the evidence on this issue below. Some rural employers do provide some in-house training, but it tends to be for very specific skills that have a limited impact on productivity and worker mobility. In the following section, I discuss some of the constraints that rural employers face in training their workforce for the future.

OBSTACLES TO EMPLOYER-PROVIDED TRAINING

In 1991, the US Department of Agriculture (USDA) published *Education and Rural Economic Development*, a report that claimed that 'despite the amount of money spent, little is known about the efficacy of employer training, and many feel it is inadequate. Training undertaken or sponsored by rural employers is unknown, but is likely to be quite low' (USDA 1991: 10). Ruy Teixeira and David McGranahan (1998) found that more than 60 percent of rural workers do not receive any training.

Rural employers face several obstacles in increasing their employee training. The most common reason employers provide for not training workers is cost. Training costs are typically viewed as nonessential and when firms need to cut costs, training is usually the first to go. Because many rural employers are small, these costs are disproportionately high and the firms do not have the infrastructure to provide in-house training.

For many rural employers, the high turnover among workers is a disincentive to invest much in job training. If employers provide job training, workers may take those new skills to another employer who will reward them with higher wages. When employers do provide training, it is often firm-specific, making it less advantageous to other employers. Under conditions of a labor surplus, employers may decide it is less costly to keep training costs to a minimum and replace workers more often. Employers with high turnover rates fail typically to underestimate the hidden costs to their business.

Some employers are just philosophically opposed to providing job training. It is the responsibility of individuals, they argue, to pay for training and education. They point to the plethora of government programs that will help subsidize training for workers. These arguments, however, are fairly short sighted. Workers often face serious obstacles, such as financial constraints, child care and transportation that prevent them from obtaining additional formal training or education. Defining job training as a personal rather than public problem fails to recognize the public welfare generated through improved training and education.

Employers frequently report that workers lack motivation for training. There may be something to these perceptions. Several studies have shown that the returns to human capital are lower in rural areas than they are in urban areas (Beaulieu and Mulkey 1995; Greenberg *et al.* 1995). The difference in the return to human capital between urban and rural areas is due largely to the lack of job opportunities in many rural areas which limits the potential of workers to find jobs that use the skills or experience they have. Rural workers may not invest in additional training for their job (or for potential, future jobs) because of the relatively low rate of return on this investment. This issue may be especially important for workers who are very attached to their community. The opportunities for training and advancement in many rural areas may be limited by the types of industries that are likely to locate in rural areas. So, it is difficult to separate out the effects of motivation versus the structure of opportunities. Clearly the two are related.

Another factor is the cost disadvantage in rural areas (Swaim 1995). The National Center on Education and the Economy reports that about 90 percent of all private sector training expenditures in the United States are made by one-half of one percent of US companies – and two-thirds of that goes to college-educated employees, who arguably need it the least (Marshall and Tucker 1992: 69). Most of these very large firms are located in metropolitan areas. In addition, urban employers can collaborate to spread the costs across several firms and reduce some of the uncertainty that workers may change jobs once they receive the training. These options may be less viable in rural areas because of the smaller number of employers with similar training needs in a region. Most small employers do not have enough resources to send their workers to a training facility or to bring training providers inside the firm. This leads to an accessibility issue concerning training providers (Teixeira and McGranahan 1998). This issue is probably much more important for rural than urban communities. Teixeira and McGranahan (1998) found that when firms were in a county with a two-year college, labor quality was less of a problem for firms.

Finally, a factor in the training gap between urban and rural areas may be the number of other employers in the region that offer jobs with similar skills. Employers are usually concerned that their trained workers will be poached by other employers with similar training needs. Thus, they are caught in a collective action problem – there is a collective need for skilled workers but individual firms may not be willing to make the investment.

In many regions, community-based organizations have emerged as key labor market intermediaries that provide an institutional response to these collective action problems and assist employers in overcoming the obstacles they face in provide job training. In the next section, I briefly review how community-based organizations are contributing to workforce development in the US.

COMMUNITY-BASED APPROACHES

Much of the literature on job training has focused on either workplace training or formal training through technical colleges or other training institutions. Only a few studies have examined the networks among training institutions, employers and community-based organizations (CBOs) (Fitzgerald 1998; Molina 1998). One major exception is a study conducted by Bennett Harrison and Marcus Weiss (1998). They studied the emergence of inter-organizational and collaborative networks across the US. Harrison and Weiss found that community development corporations (CDCs) and other CBOs have become essential actors in workforce development networks. Although their exploration of networks focused on metropolitan cases, I believe this approach may have some critical advantages to overcoming the resistance to training by employers in rural areas. For example, CBOs may help solve the collective action problem in training by bringing together several firms to collaborate on training efforts (Melendez and Harrison 1998). If several firms with similar training needs work together, there is less likelihood that individual firms will lose their investment in training. Similarly, by pooling resources, employers may be able to reduce some of the costs to providing training.

Community-based approaches to workforce development also may rely more heavily on in-house programs than technical colleges or other institutions. Community-based organizations may solve some of the problems unique to rural areas because they help match workers to available jobs, thus removing some of the disincentives rural workers face in obtaining additional training.

Harrison and Weiss (1998) identify three distinct structures of workforce development networks. Hub-spoke employment networks have a community-based organization (CBO) at the center of the network that links employers, trainers and public officials. The San Jose-based Center for Employment Training (CET) and Project QUEST in San Antonio are examples of this model.

The second model is the peer-to-peer workforce development networks, which consist of several CBOs linked together at the core of the network. Examples of this model include the Chicago Jobs Council, the Pittsburgh Partnership for Neighborhood Development and the Business Outreach Centers of New York City.

Finally, in some cases a regional training institution may play a central role in the network, referred to as an intermediary training network, and is linked with other CBOs to provide training. Examples of intermediary training networks include the Regional Alliance of Small Contractors in New Jersey.

Harrison and Weiss's analysis is largely descriptive and does not provide any explanation of how these different institutional structures might influence the breadth and depth of job training provided by employers. They provide little information on how workforce development networks are initiated, their effectiveness, and their ability to elicit employer participation. This research will begin to answer some of these basic questions. The research design provides a holistic understanding of these networks by collecting information from employers, training institutions and the CBOs involved. By holistic, I mean that I will look at the motivations and experiences of employers, community colleges and CBOs that have been involved in workforce development networks. I hope this approach provides a better understanding of how and why the various actors participate in these networks.

Although we know some of the obstacles to increasing employer training, we still do not know much about how firms make decisions about training. Neither do we have a good understanding of what it will take to help low-wage employers in rural areas increase their productivity, as well as wages and benefits. Understanding the process, opening up the black box to see what is inside, rather than focusing on training inputs and outputs, can provide us information about the factors that firms use in deciding whether or not they provide training, how it is offered, who provides it, who participates, and when training is offered. Knowing more about the actual decision-making process may assist policy-makers in designing federal and state workforce development programs that facilitate productivity increases and ultimately wages in rural areas.

Because a comprehensive theory of job training is non-existent (Knoke and Kalleberg 1994) and human capital theories use the individual as their unit of analysis (Beaulieu and Mulkey 1995), we cannot simply use these theoretical models to explain firm behavior. Human capital theory places the burden of education and training responsibility on the individual. The firm in these theories has no responsibility towards their community or their workers. We need to develop better explanations of firm behavior as it relates to training specifically and to human capital development generally. The context for these investments should matter as well. Because of the low density of employers in rural areas and the difficulty in matching demand with supply, theories that are used in urban settings may not be as effective in rural areas.

THE STUDY

This study focuses on the creation, organization and effectiveness of workforce development networks in rural areas. I employ several data sets, including surveys of employers and training institutions, as well as intensive case studies of workforce development networks in rural areas across the US. By using mixed methods to examine these issues, I believe I am able to overcome some of the weaknesses inherent in any single method. This approach also permits me to assess the validity and reliability of key measures and concepts. In addition, I also use data triangulation by collecting data from the various actors involved in workforce development networks. In this regard, I go beyond previous studies that only look at a single component of a workforce development network. There is a substantial literature looking exclusively at employer patterns, some research has examined community colleges and only a few studies have analyzed the role of CBOs in job training. Yet, there has been no attempt to understand how these various parts relate to one another and how they might influence the actions of others. I consider several subsets of questions that are related to workforce development networks in rural areas:

1. How do firms make decisions about employee training? What factors contribute to investments in training? Are there different influences on the type of training (short-term versus continuous, specific versus general, and so on)? What factors influence the length of training and when it is provided? How does collaboration influence the breadth and depth of employer-provided training?

2. How do programs available at community colleges and other training institutions influence employer investments in training? Are community colleges providing the broad skills workers need or are they responding to employer needs to provide firm or industry specific training? How well do community colleges work with community-based organizations and other institutions involved in workforce development networks? How does involvement in these networks influence their training programs?

3. Can community-based organizations (CBOs) help employers overcome the obstacles to improved training efforts? In particular, can community-based training efforts reduce some of the uncertainty that employers face in their investment in training and the costs of these programs? Does the existence of community-based training efforts improve the process of matching the supply and demand of labor in the region?

This book is organized into six chapters. In Chapter 2 I examine the structure and change in rural labor markets. I pay special attention to the major industrial and occupation changes in rural America since the 1980s. I discuss the role of social networks in the functioning of labor markets and how government training programs have lacked the ties to employers and training institutions in rural communities.

Chapter 3 draws from an employer survey I conducted of businesses in nonmetropolitan areas of the US. In this chapter I focus on the levels and types of employer-provided training in these regions. I also look at the extent to which employers collaborate with community-based organizations and other institutions in coordinating workforce development, and the effects on job training.

In Chapter 4 I analyze data from a survey of community colleges serving businesses in nonmetropolitan areas. I explore how community colleges balance the pressures to provide traditional classroom instruction with the demands of regional businesses for customized training programs. I also assess their involvement with community-based organizations and their effects on programs and services offered through these institutions.

Chapter 5 summarizes my case studies of three community-based organizations involved in job training in nonmetropolitan areas. The case studies reveal some interesting differences in organizational structure and in the way CBOs structure employer participation.

In Chapter 6 I discuss the implications of this study for public policy and community development. I also review some of the lessons learned from the workforce development efforts that have been successful in rural areas.

NOTE

1. Throughout this book, I will use the terms rural and nonmetropolitan interchangeably. In the US, rural is officially defined as a municipality or other area with fewer than 2500 people. Metropolitan areas are defined as a municipality with 50 000 or more people and including neighboring counties with high numbers of commuters. It is possible that some rural areas are in metropolitan regions and nonmetropolitan areas have some urban municipalities. For the most part, however, the two terms can be used in a similar way.

2.   Rural labor markets, networks and workforce development

Employment in rural America was once dominated by jobs in extractive industries, such as agriculture, forestry, mining and fishing. Today, most rural workers earn their wages in manufacturing and service industries. Although rural labor markets look more like urban labor markets, some important differences remain. In this chapter I review some of the key differences between rural and urban labor markets. In the second part of the chapter I examine several broad strategies for building rural labor markets. Supply-side approaches tend to emphasize human capital development through education and training. Demand-side approaches focus on increasing the number of high skilled jobs and opportunities for advancement. Institutional approaches stress organizational features that influence the functioning of labor markets. I discuss these strategies in the context of rural labor markets and their implications for job training in rural America. I pay special attention to the growing body of literature that emphasizes the important role of social networks in local labor markets. Finally, I analyze the changing context for workforce development in rural areas. Several policy changes, such as the Workforce Investment Act, have important implications for how workforce training is now organized.

CONDITIONS IN RURAL AND URBAN LABOR MARKETS

Probably one of the most noted differences in rural and urban labor markets is the gap in educational attainment between metropolitan and nonmetropolitan areas. This gap is especially large when we examine the percentage of the population 25 years or older who are college graduates. In 2000, approximately 27 percent of metropolitan residents 25 years or older were college graduates, while only 16 percent of nonmetropolitan residents had attained a college degree. The gap is increasing, at least for the number of college graduates (Table 2.1). In 1970 only 11.6 percent of metropolitan residents held a college degree, while 7 percent of nonmetropolitan residents did. Conversely, while there is a persistent gap in the percentage of residents

Table 2.1   Metropolitan and nonmetropolitan educational attainment, 1960–2000 (persons 25 years old and over)

Year	Less than high school		High school graduate		Some college		College graduate	
	Metropolitan (%)	Nonmetro (%)	Metropolitan (%)	Nonmetro (%)	Metropolitan (%)	Nonmetro (%)	Metropolitan (%)	Nonmetro (%)
1960	56.8	66.1	25.5	21.7	9.2	7.1	8.5	5.1
1970	45.4	55.9	31.8	28.6	11.2	8.5	11.6	7.0
1980	31.3	41.7	34.5	35.0	16.5	12.5	17.7	10.8
1990	23.1	31.2	28.7	34.8	25.9	21.2	22.3	12.8
2000	18.7	23.2	26.9	35.5	27.8	25.7	26.6	15.5

Source: Economic Research Service, US Department of Agriculture. Retrieved from www.ers.usda.gov/Briefing/LaborAndEducation/Table_1.htm (accessed 6 January 2004).

13

in metropolitan and nonmetropolitan areas that have not completed a high school degree, the gap is closing. Although 5 percent more nonmetropolitan residents had not completed high school than metropolitan residents in 2000, the gap was more than 10 percent in 1970.

One explanation for the educational attainment differences is the age structure of the populations in metropolitan and nonmetropolitan areas. Because nonmetropolitan areas have a higher percentage of older residents, and older residents tend to have completed less schooling than younger ones, nonmetropolitan areas on average have less educational attainment. The data suggest, however, that the gap persists at all age levels, although it is less for younger residents. There are some significant regional differences in this gap in educational attainment between metropolitan and nonmetro-politan areas. The South has the most disadvantaged nonmetropolitan areas in terms of educational attainment.

Another factor in this gap may be educational quality. A frequently used measure of educational quality is student reading and mathematics perform-ance on standardized tests. One source of standardized data to compare rural and urban students is the National Assessment of Educational Progress (NAEP), which was given to fourth and eighth graders in 2003 (US Department of Education 2005). Based on these data, students in rural schools are more likely to perform above the basic level on these assessments than are students in metropolitan areas. In 2003, 20 percent of the fourth grade students in rural schools scored below the basic level for mathematics, while 33 percent of the students in all central city schools and 38 percent of students in large central city schools were below the basic level. The gap in mathematics scores among rural and urban students actually increased a bit by the eighth grade. With regard to reading assessments, 34 percent of the fourth grade students in rural schools failed to achieve the basic level, while 49 percent of the central city students and 55 percent of the central city stu-dents in large schools were below the basic level. This gap narrowed some-what by the eighth grade. By the eighth grade, only 25 percent of rural students were scoring below the basic level, while 37 percent of central city students and 43 percent of central city students in large schools had scores below the basic level. Thus, it does not appear that performance on stan-dardized tests contributes to the lower levels of human capital in rural areas. In fact, rural schools, on average, do better than urban ones on most stan-dardized measures of achievement.

Another plausible explanation is that the types of educational programs and services offered may contribute to the educational differences in rural versus urban schools. Smaller enrollments in rural areas may mean that these schools are not able to provide as wide of a variety of programs as urban schools. The US Department of Education (2003) reports that rural schools are less likely than urban schools to offer programs for fast-growing occupations, such as computer graphic designers, computer programmers or medical assistants. Instead, rural schools are more likely to offer vocational programs in traditional semi-skilled positions. Also, rural schools typically cannot offer as many foreign language programs or specialized courses simply because of their small size. It may be that the lack of programs in such areas as foreign language and specialized math and science courses may place rural students at a disadvantage in college. There seems to be a very limited body of literature on this issue, however.

Teachers in rural areas generally get paid less than those in urban areas. In the academic year 1999–2000 teachers in rural/small town areas earned approximately $37 000 while teachers in central cities earned more than $44 000 (US Department of Education 2006). More qualified teachers may be attracted to urban areas because of the higher salaries. Although teachers in rural areas have lower salaries, they are less likely to move to another school or leave teaching altogether (US Department of Education 2006).

Overall expenditures per student also tend to vary by community size. In the school year 2003–4, total expenditures per student in large cities was $8661, while the figure was around $7500 for rural areas (US Department of Education 2003). As one might expect, the pupil/teacher ratio tends to be lower in rural than in urban areas, which might help explain some of the differences in the performance on standardized tests.

As I discussed in the first chapter, the internet has become an increasingly important source of information for rural residents, and is increasingly used for instruction purposes. A recent survey conducted by the US Department of Education (2004) found that almost all schools in urban and rural areas have access to the internet. There are some differences in the number of computers with access to the internet per student, however. In large cities, there are about 5.5 students per computer with internet access, while the ratio is about 4.4 in rural areas.

There is a growing body of literature suggesting that students that attend preschools perform better once they start school. Rural areas may be disadvantaged in providing these experiences for children.

Overall, the evidence regarding educational quality in rural and urban areas is mixed. Clearly, rural areas lack the resources to provide many of the services that urban schools can provide. At the same time, rural schools tend to offer smaller class sizes, lower teacher turnover and higher performance on standardized exams. For many rural schools today, the critical challenge is keeping a sufficient size to resist consolidation.

Next, I would like to turn to several issues related to employment in rural and urban labor markets. Employment growth rates in metropolitan and nonmetropolitan areas now follow very similar patterns. Throughout much of the early 1990s, rates of employment growth were somewhat lower in metropolitan areas than in nonmetropolitan regions. As the economic expansion took off in the mid-1990s, employment growth in metropolitan areas was considerably higher than in nonmetropolitan areas. This pattern changed abruptly with the recession of 2001–2. Employment growth in metropolitan areas has been lower than in nonmetropolitan areas since the recession. Many resource-dependent communities were not as affected by the recession because they did not have many manufacturing jobs. Nonmetropolitan areas experienced a larger loss of manufacturing jobs during this period.

The percentage of the population that is employed, what is referred to as the employed/population ratio, tends to be lower in nonmetropolitan than in metropolitan areas. The advantage of this measure of labor force participation, compared to the unemployment rate, is that it takes into consideration individuals who are not currently searching for work (such as discouraged workers, individuals in school, etc.). The gap in the employed/population ratio has remained relatively constant over the past decades with metropolitan areas maintaining about a 4 percent higher ratio. One of the reasons for this gap is the older population in nonmetropolitan areas. Additionally, more traditional ideas about the role of women may influence their labor force participation rates. The gap is undoubtedly influenced by the relatively low wages in many rural areas as well. Many women, especially those with young children, may not be able to find jobs that pay enough to justify entering the labor market. Access to and cost of child care and transportation costs also may be serious obstacles for many families.

As has already been suggested, the occupational and industrial structure of metropolitan and nonmetropolitan areas look quite different. Table 2.2 presents the percentage of the labor force in major occupational categories. As can be seen, metropolitan areas have a higher percentage of managerial jobs, as well as service and office positions. Nonmetropolitan areas have a higher percentage of extraction and production jobs.

Research suggests that underemployment rates vary across metropolitan and nonmetropolitan areas. Lichter and Costanzo (1987) used the 1980 Current Population Survey to show that nonmetropolitan rates of underemployment are much higher, largely due to the lower rates of education in nonmetropolitan than in metropolitan areas. Similarly, Jensen *et al.* (1999) find that nonmetropolitan workers are more likely to be underemployed and are less likely to become adequately employed than metropolitan workers. They also find that the gap between nonmetropolitan and metropolitan workers increases with relevant statistical controls.

The tight labor markets and economic expansion of the 1990s led to rapid increases in wages and salaries for most workers, especially low-income and

Table 2.2 Percentage of workers in occupational category by metropolitan and nonmetropolitan areas, 2000

Inside and outside Metropolitan area	Management, professional, and related occupations	Service occupations	Sales and office occupations	Farming, fishing and forestry occupations	Construction, extraction, and maintenance occupations	Production, transportation, and material moving occupations
In metropolitan area	35.2	14.6	27.5	0.5	8.9	13.3
In central city	34.3	16.8	27.2	0.3	7.9	13.4
Not in central city	35.7	13.4	27.6	0.5	9.5	13.2
Urban	36.9	13.4	28.3	0.4	8.7	12.4
In urbanized area	37.6	13.2	28.5	0.3	8.5	11.9
In urban cluster	28	16.5	25.5	1.8	10.7	17.6
Rural	30.6	13.1	24.8	1.3	13.1	17.2
Not in metropolitan area	26.9	15.9	23.2	1.9	11.7	20.4
Urban	27.5	17.9	24.8	1.1	9.7	18.9
In urbanized area	31	16.6	25.8	0.8	9.4	16.3
In urban cluster	27	18.1	24.6	1.2	9.8	19.3
Rural	26.4	14.7	22.1	2.4	13.1	21.4

Notes:
GCT-P13. Occupation, Industry, and Class of Worker of Employed Civilians 16 Years and Over: 2000.
Data Set: Census 2000 Summary File 3 (SF 3) – Sample Data.
Geographic Area: United States – Inside/Outside Metropolitan Area.
Detailed Occupation Code List (PDF 42KB).

Source: US Census Bureau, Census 2000 Summary File 3, Matrices P49, P50, and P51.

minority workers. Rates of growth in earnings were very similar in metropolitan and nonmetropolitan areas. Since the recession of 2000, the rate of
earnings growth has slowed, but the growth rate has fallen much more in
metropolitan regions of the US. These conclusions tend to be consistent
with the discussion earlier about employment growth across metropolitan
and nonmetropolitan areas. Overall, it appears that the recession was especially harsh in metropolitan regions that had a relatively large manufacturing base. On average, nonmetropolitan areas did not experience the same
level of restructuring. It should be recognized, however, that many counties
in nonmetropolitan areas are dependent on manufacturing employment,
especially in the South and Midwest, and these areas did see significant
employment losses and lower gains in employment during the recession.

Poverty rates have mirrored the changes in employment and income
growth rates. Poverty rates declined through the 1990s, especially for
minorities. The poverty rate dropped faster in metropolitan than in nonmetropolitan areas. Also, the poverty rate began increasing in both metropolitan and nonmetropolitan areas during the recession, but metropolitan
rates have climbed faster.

Overall, the evidence suggests that both metropolitan and nonmetropolitan labor markets respond to national, and even international, economic
forces. Historically there has been a gap between metropolitan and nonmetropolitan labor markets with respect to economic and social well-being.
Nonmetropolitan areas have generally lagged behind metropolitan areas in
employment and income growth. There have been several recent periods,
however, when nonmetropolitan labor markets have been advantaged relative
to metropolitan areas. It is difficult to identify the causal factors of this rever-
sal in fortunes. The answer probably lies in the interaction between external
forces (for example economic expansion/recession, global competition, and
technological change) with local labor market structures (for example local
labor supply, level of human capital, and regional industry structure). Below,
I identify some of the major structural changes in nonmetropolitan labor
markets that ultimately may affect the well-being of residents in these areas.

STRUCTURAL CHANGES IN RURAL LABOR MARKETS

Although one could identify several important changes in rural labor
markets, I focus on the shift from extractive and manufacturing to service
sector employment and the associated changes in the demand for skills in
nonmetropolitan labor market areas. These changes seem to be having the
most dramatic effects on rural labor markets.

Sectoral Shifts in Production

Although much of the literature on economic restructuring has focused on urban areas, nonmetropolitan regions also have experienced a shift from the manufacturing to the service economy. Farming, mining and timber industries have undergone considerable downsizing over the last several decades, resulting in declining employment opportunities in the traditional economic base of nonmetropolitan localities. Rural America experienced an 'industrial invasion' during the 1970s, but in the 1980s manufacturing growth slowed. In contrast, service sector industries have experienced steady employment growth in nonmetropolitan areas. By 1996, service sector industries accounted for 68.4 percent of all nonmetropolitan jobs, compared to 16.3 percent for the manufacturing sector and 6.6 percent in farming.

Some have argued that technological change and improved transportation systems would facilitate the growth of the service sector in rural America (Allen and Dillman 1994). It was anticipated that service employment would decentralize to rural areas, much like manufacturing employment did during the 1960s and 1970s. Research suggests, however, this has not happened (Glasmeier and Howland 1995). Although the service sector has grown in rural areas, higher paying jobs in the service sector have largely remained in urban areas. The largest share of nonmetropolitan service sector growth has occurred in social services (especially health services) and government. While employment in producer services has expanded at a lower rate in nonmetropolitan counties compared to metropolitan counties, the most rapidly expanding major industry group in the entire service sector in nonmetropolitan counties was business services.

Research on the effects of the growth of the service sector is mixed. Metropolitan-based services have been found to provide higher earnings than in nonmetropolitan areas (Stanback and Noyelle 1982). Leann Tigges and Deborah Tootle (1990) found employment in peripheral service industries to be positively related to unemployment and the number of part-time jobs among white males in rural labor market areas.[1] They also found, however, that concentration of employment in peripheral service industries was negatively associated with low-wage employment.

Another reason that the shift to the service sector may affect rural areas is because it is often accompanied by a shift toward small firms. The literature on this topic suggests that there may be both benefits and costs associated with the shift toward small firms. Charles Brown *et al.* (1990) found that workers in small firms receive lower wages and have fewer benefits. Recent research on small manufacturing firms and locality well-being in nonmetropolitan areas, however, indicates a positive relationship

(Lyson and Tolbert 1996; Tolbert *et al.* 1998). Growth of small manufacturing may have more benefits than growth in the number of small service
establishments. Small establishments often provide more opportunities for
growth and are more innovative, which often has benefits for the region's
economy.

There may be some important differences between nonmetropolitan
and metropolitan areas with regard to the restructuring process. Firms in
nonmetropolitan areas tend to be later in the profit/product cycle than
those in metropolitan areas (Markusen 1987). Innovative and high profit
firms are most likely to be located in metropolitan areas where they have
access to producer services, large consumer markets, and linkages with
other firms in their industry. This means that nonmetropolitan firms tend
to be later in the profit cycle may be more vulnerable to global competition
than are firms in metropolitan areas. For example, Frank Romo and
Michael Schwartz (1995) found that while location decisions among core
firms are influenced by outside competition, peripheral firms are more
dependent on the material, political, and social resources available in the
local production culture. We would expect the rate of economic restructuring to be higher in nonmetropolitan areas, and the loss of branch plants to
have a greater effect on the restructuring process than would be the case in
metropolitan areas (Glasmeier *et al.* 1995).

Shift in Demand for Skills

There has been a growing debate in the social sciences over the extent to
which the demand for skills has changed in the economy. A large body of
economic literature suggests there has been a marked shift in employer
demand away from less-educated workers and a growing shortage in the
number of skilled workers (Holzer 1991). Most of the explanations for this
skills mismatch point to technological advances, especially computer technology, and growing international competition as the forces which have
devalued low-skilled work in the United States (Krueger 1993). Even in the
jobs that continue to be filled by low-skilled workers, employers are
demanding an increasingly complex set of social skills due to organizational changes and the need to interact with customers (Kirschenman and
Neckerman 1991).

To what an extent are nonmetropolitan areas facing a skills mismatch?
The evidence on this issue is not clear. As I have already suggested, the level
of education and training in rural areas continue to lag behind urban areas.
Ruy Teixeira and David McGranahan (1998) analyzed data from a manufacturing survey conducted by the Economic Research Service and found
that while employers were demanding more skills, only a small number were

adopting new technology and requiring a more educated workforce. David McGranahan and Linda Ghelfi (1998) suggest, however, that rural manu-facturers may have begun adopting more complex technology and rely more heavily on skilled workers in the 1990s. None of this research, however, has assessed directly the changing demand for skills among service firms in rural areas. In a more recent study, Gibbs *et al.* (2004) argue that to understand what is happening to low-skill employment, we need to take into consideration both industry and occupational change. They find that the shift to service sector employment has lowered the proportion of low-skilled jobs in rural areas. They demonstrate that there has been a marked shift toward more skilled occupations within industries that has contributed to these changes. Labor market conditions also may make it difficult to assess the extent to which a skills mismatch exists. In periods of high unemployment, employers may seek workers who have more skills than they actually need. In a labor shortage, they may be more inclined to search for workers with the basic skills they need.

There may be several reasons for a skill gap in nonmetropolitan areas (Gibbs *et al.* 1998). First, the returns to education and training in rural areas tend to be lower than they are in urban areas. The lower returns are primarily due to the more limited opportunities for employment in rural areas. Thus, rural workers may be more reluctant to invest in training to obtain a better job. Second, firms located in rural areas tend to provide less formal job training because of costs and they tend to be later in the profit cycle than firms in urban areas. As a result, there may be few opportunities for mobility within rural firms. Finally, lower rates of unionization in rural areas also means that apprenticeships and other similar programs for developing skilled workers are less likely to exist.

Globalization, technological change and regional shifts in production have all contributed to the restructuring of jobs in metropolitan and non-metropolitan areas. Economic restructuring may have influenced the quantity and the quality of jobs that remain (Tilly 1996). Many critics charge that the quality of jobs has declined significantly over the past 25 years. They contend that these processes have contributed to the growth in the number of part-time and temporary jobs and the growing practice of out-sourcing (Tilly 1996).

Although globalization may eliminate many jobs, those that remain may be high wage, high skilled positions that are not exposed to the same level of foreign competition. Globalization, however, may put pressure on high wage jobs. It is also important to consider the variation within industrial sectors with respect to global competition and import penetration. Some sectors may not be influenced by global competition and the consequences for workers in these sectors may be quite different.

The same questions can be raised about the effects of technological change. Technological advances, especially computerization, have increased productivity and job loss throughout the economy. Some critics have argued that technological change has led to a deskilling process that lowers the quality of jobs, and ultimately pushes wages and benefits to lower levels. Much of the evidence suggests, however, that the skills demanded for many jobs have increased significantly.

Overall, the literature is unclear as to the consequences of globalization and technological change for low-wage workers in rural areas. Are these processes leading to a race to the bottom or an upgrading of skills? Unfortunately, there is very little data to answer these questions and to understand the different responses to restructuring in rural areas.

There has been much debate in recent years about the potential of shifting jobs to a knowledge economy based on a 'creative class' (Florida 2002). Some of this optimism waned after the high tech bubble burst in 2000. Yet, may policy analysts continue to advocate strategies that promote jobs requiring high levels of education and creativity. What are the prospects of rural areas benefiting from these strategies? There may be a few success stories, but very little evidence of a significant transformation in rural areas toward a knowledge economy. Creation of a knowledge class may rely on amenities and institutions that rarely exist in rural areas. Richard Florida (2002) identifies the necessary ingredients for a creative class – technology, talent and tolerance – all of which tend to be lacking in rural areas. Although Florida's analysis has been criticized by many academic social scientists, policy-makers and local leaders have been intrigued with the prospects of creating a knowledge economy that would generate higher paying jobs that are less vulnerable to low cost areas of the global economy. Yet, there are many obstacles to achieving these goals. Many rural areas continue to lack broadband access that would permit residents access to new technology. In some states, municipalities have been blocked from providing these services. Similarly, most rural areas are not in close proximity to universities or colleges, which provide much of the labor, technology and innovation for the knowledge economy. Finally, rural communities often lack the openness and tolerance that would allow a creative class to flourish. Many of these obstacles could be overcome, but would require both local and state initiatives that address these problems. Although the concept of the knowledge economy is an attractive one, most rural communities face structural and institutional obstacles that need to be overcome. The rather simplistic policy recommendations that have been made are inadequate to move rural areas toward this goal of increasing the number of jobs in the knowledge economy.

LABOR MARKET THEORIES

Labor market theories tend to fall into one of three groups: supply-, demand- or institutionally-oriented theories. Most theories recognize the importance of all these factors. Each, however, recommends policy intervention on a different side of the labor market.

Supply-side theories emphasize productivity as a major factor influencing labor supply. Productivity is largely a function of skills, knowledge and experience acquired by workers. Supply-side approaches to intervening in local labor markets stress the importance of education and training programs as a means of increasing productivity and ultimately workers' earnings. Historically, supply-side policies have been aimed directly at low-income workers. Examples of supply-side policies are subsidies to workers, such as the Earned Income Tax Credit, or subsidies for work-related expenses, such as child care. Bartik (2001) argues that most American labor market policies have used this approach.

Demand-side theories emphasize the importance of job creation as a means of creating opportunities in the local labor market. Demand-side policies are directed at changing the behavior of employers or in providing public sector jobs. Examples of demand-side policies include wage subsidies to employers for hiring targeted workers or economic development policies that provide incentives for employers to create new jobs for workers. Employers in rural areas have less demand for skilled workers and tend to be located in competitive markets that pressure them to cut costs, especially for job training. Thus, government policy has focused on generating public employment in many rural areas as a means of building the local labor market.

Institutional theories have traditionally focused on the organization of work as a mediating factor between the supply of and demand for workers. How work is organized can influence the skill mix needed in a locality, the wages and returns to investments in human capital, and other dimensions of the local labor market. For instance, firm size and industrial structure influence the returns workers receive on investments in education and training. Workers with the same level of education, training and experience in large firms tend to earn more than workers in small businesses. Unionization also is an institutional factor that can influence labor market dynamics, with workers in unionized firms earning more than workers in non-union firms, even with the same level of education, training, experience and in the same jobs and industries. Space and density are major obstacles to improving the link between the demand for and supply of labor in rural areas. In the next section of this chapter, I examine the role of networks in local labor markets. Because networks are so critical in linking workers to job opportunities, we need to understand how they influence the functioning of rural labor markets.

Networks in Labor Markets

In recent years, institutional theories have focused less on the organizational structure of firms and industries and more on how employers, training institutions, intermediaries and other actors are linked across labor markets. This literature suggests that networks are critical components of markets and that the structure of these networks can influence the way in which markets function. Research on the role of networks in labor markets has focused on several issues: the importance of networks versus formal information in the job search process; the different effects of networks among racial, gender and ethnic groups; and the effects of the structure and composition of social networks. In this section, I briefly discuss some of the ways in which networks matter across local labor markets rather than for individuals. My focus is on how these networks establish relationships between employers, training and educational institutions, workers, intermediaries and other community-based organizations.

Workforce development networks have emerged as an institutional response to several labor markets problems (Giloth 2000). First, there was recognition among practitioners and policy makers that employment training programs were not having the desired impact on family income and poverty. Most of these training efforts were supported by federally funded programs. One of the criticisms has been that training programs were not very well linked to local needs and employers had little involvement in the design of the programs. Second, the restructuring of local labor markets, especially the loss of manufacturing jobs and the decline of internal labor markets, generated more demand for training programs. Training programs were typically disconnected with one another and frequently were not available for workers who were not considered poor or disadvantaged.

Workforce development networks may improve the functioning of local labor markets in several ways. First, networks improve the flow of information to employers, workers and training institutions. Employers lack information about the productivity of potential workers, and therefore, frequently rely on signals, such as high school diplomas, to make hiring decisions (Holzer 1996). Employers also rely on their existing workers to provide information about job applicants (Granovetter 1995). Networks provide employers with a wider basis of information through community-based organizations, training institutions and other intermediaries about the work ethic and skills of workers. Most workers find jobs through informal networks. This process hurts minority workers because their social ties are likely to have very similar information about jobs (Green *et al.* 1999). Workforce development networks enable job searchers to combine informal with formal sources of information to overcome some of these problems (Melendez and Harrison 1998). For example, community-based organizations can provide more formal and broader sources of information through interorganizational ties. At the same time, they have local contacts with workers to improve the flow of information in the region. Training institutions also benefit from participating in these networks because they improve their understanding of employer and worker needs. Workforce development networks enable training institutions to better gauge the demand for workers in their region.

Floundering is a common problem among youth entering the labor market (Stern *et al.* 1994). Although there are many factors that may contribute to floundering, lack of adequate information about job requirements is considered a key. Workforce development networks can smooth this transition from school to work by improving the flow of information between educational institutions and employers. They also upgrade the basic training for the jobs available in the region by coordinating training through schools with local employers. If younger workers can see a potential path for mobility in the local labor market, they may be more likely to stay with their current employer, which has benefits for both workers and employers. As we will see in the case studies, workforce development networks often build school-to-work and apprenticeship programs that help build the connections between schools and employers.

In his seminal article on job training, Gary Becker (1962) argues that employers will not offer general training because they may lose these investments to other firms. Instead, they provide specific training that develops skills that are not as easily transferred to other employers. Employers, thus, face a collective action problem in providing job training. It is in the interests of all employers to have a well-educated and trained workforce, but it is not in the interests of individual employers to bear those costs. Small employers also face economic constraints because of economies of scale. Larger employers have several workers who need similar types of training, while small employers typically do not. Workforce development networks address these structural problems by linking employers, training institutions and community-based organizations in ways that reduce the costs and risks of employer-provided training. If several employers can be brought together to provide training through a collaborative effort, the risk and cost to individual employers is reduced. In Chapter 3, I will examine this hypothesis in more detail and assess how the structure of these collaborative efforts might influence employer-provided training.

Establishing collaborative networks also can improve the paths of mobility within the local labor market. By linking employers with different levels of skill needs, workforce development networks can create career ladders. Historically, the path of mobility for workers has been within firms. As a worker gained experience and training, he/she would be promoted to positions with more responsibility and pay. That model, however, is less likely to exist in firms today. Many employers hire skilled workers from the outside. Thus, the full responsibility of obtaining training is placed on the individual worker. Most workers face dead-end jobs with their employer and must change jobs to improve their livelihood. One strategy for increasing the likelihood that workers can gain experiences and skills leading to higher-paying jobs is to establish clear paths of mobility among employers in the local labor market (Dresser 2000). Low-skill employers profit from these networks because it reduces their turnover rates and employers demanding higher levels of skills benefit because they have a pool of skilled workers from which they can draw. Workforce development networks can build paths of mobility within local labor markets that existed in large firms in the past.

Workforce development networks can help promote industrial clusters (Porter 2000). By bringing together firms in an industry and identifying common skill needs and other areas of collaboration, workforce development networks construct an infrastructure that attracts other businesses that may support the cluster or firms that have similar needs (Rosenfeld 2001).

Workforce development networks face numerous obstacles, especially in rural areas. Employer participation is frequently a major problem. There are several reasons for their lack of participation, including time, cost, and few perceived benefits. Small businesses, in particular, have fewer resources to devote to and obtain fewer benefits from these collaborative efforts.

Social networks tend to work best when actors have a wide range of contacts. In Mark Granovetter's (1995) path-breaking work on the role of social networks in labor markets, he found that job searchers were most successful when they used friends of friends (weak ties) to find a job. Job searchers who rely on close family, friends or neighbors (strong ties) have a narrower range of information available to them. What may be especially disadvantageous is using what sociologists refer to as multiplex relationships – friends or family who are also neighbors or coworkers. Minorities and women are more likely to rely on these types of networks and they help explain their wage disadvantage (Green *et al.* 1999). Much of the research has found that the structure of social networks varies across the urban-rural divide (Beggs *et al.* 1996). Nonmetropolitan residents still have stronger ties to family, friends and neighbors than do metropolitan residents, and they rely more heavily on these strong ties in searching for work.

It may be more difficult to initiate and implement workforce development programs in rural areas because of these dense networks. Ironically, they may work more effectively in urban areas where it may be easier to bridge various networks, organizations and institutions.

The thinness of rural labor markets presents some unique obstacles to workforce development. The number of workers with similar training needs is smaller in rural than urban areas which makes it difficult for educational and training institutions to develop appropriate programs. In an urban area, the demand for welders, for example, would be so high that educational institutions can justify the startup expense and employers will be hiring several workers with these skills. In rural areas, the demand is much thinner. The thin demand for skilled and professional workers also limits the options of job seekers and ultimately affects the wage levels available in those positions.

Finally, the low population density in rural areas makes communication across communities and organizations very difficult. In most urban areas, employers, training institutions, and community-based organizations are in close proximity to one another, which helps facilitate communication and coordination. Community colleges and training institutions in rural areas serve a much broader region, which often limits the amount of interaction they have with employers, local governments or other community groups. The size of community colleges and training institutions is also smaller than in urban areas, which restricts the size and diversity of programs they can offer in these areas.

THE CONTEXT FOR WORKFORCE DEVELOPMENT

Historically, the United States has relied primarily on a market-based system for matching workers to jobs. This system relies on workers making investments in training and education that will enhance their skills and job prospects. The assumption in this system is that workers have adequate information on job opportunities in the region or will be willing to move to regions that have more job opportunities. Employer-provided training is not a primary tool for improving the productivity of the workforce.

To improve the opportunities of disadvantaged workers, the federal government has provided several training programs. For example, the Comprehensive Employment and Training Act of 1973 (CETA) established support for unemployed and underemployed workers. This program was replaced by the Job Training Partnership Act (JTPA) of 1982. The program was less centralized than CETA and provided Private Industry Councils (PICs) with the ability to coordinate programs among training institutions, unions and employers. As I pointed out earlier, these programs have been heavily criticized for their duplication and the lack of responsiveness to local demand.

In 2003, the General Accounting Office identified 44 federal programs providing employment training services (GAO 2003). Two agencies – the Department of Education and the Department of Labor – offered about two-thirds of these programs. All the federal programs served more than 30 million participants. Total funding for these programs exceeds $30 billion. The services provided range from employment counseling and assessment to support services like child care and occupational or vocational training. Many of the programs focus on economically disadvantaged workers.

In response to many of these critiques, these programs were recently replaced by the Workforce Investment Act of 1998. This Act now replaces the PICs with Workforce Investment Boards that encourage more private sector involvement in training activities. In an attempt to be more responsive, the Act requires active involvement of employers and government officials. The goal is to consolidate coordinate, and improve employment, training, literacy and vocational rehabilitation programs in the United States. The Act promotes a 'one-stop' approach to training and employment programs that is managed at the local level. Over 800 centers have been established to provide a single point of contact for employers and workers to obtain services. The Act attempts to promote greater accountability and flexibility in training programs. For example, as part of the Workforce Investment Act, the federal government has established 'training accounts' that permit workers to purchase the training that best meets their needs. Each workforce development area is administered by a board that is required to establish a strategic plan for its region.

The Workforce Investment Act has made great strides in providing more coherence to the employment and training system in the United States. Yet, it still has many limitations. Relatively few employers and workers are using the system. Workers continue to rely heavily on informal networks to obtain information about job openings. Employers have not found the system very useful. They also use informal search methods, such as their existing workforce, to find qualified job seekers. Employers also complain that the system does not provide any pre-employment training or use any filtering processes that would improve the match between the opportunities and workers. The Workforce Investment Act attempts to provide greater coordination of regional training employment programs through a formal bureaucratic structure. It does very little to encourage the Boards to reach out to community-based organizations that could help implement these programs. It is essentially the same actors that have been involved in regional training activities in the past. Finally, I would question whether the

Workforce Investment Act has improved employer participation in the formation and implementation of training and employment programs. As is often the case, it is primarily the largest employers in the region that are participating in the workforce development boards.

Winton Pitcoff (1998) argues that the Workforce Investment Act presents some challenges to community-based development organizations involved in workforce development networks. Much of the money has gone to for-profit trainers that are not run by the same principles as nonprofit organizations. It will be difficult for nonprofit organizations to compete against these for-profit trainers because of the emphasis on strict performance standards. Community-based organizations are more inclined to take on tougher cases and to deal with a broader set of worker issues. For-profit organizations do very little to address neighborhood needs and to help workers gain access to a broader set of services.

In many regions, the Workforce Investment Act has done very little to change how training and employment services are provided. It established 'one-stop' shops, but this innovation had already been implemented in many states. Many of the actors were the same and it did not do a significantly better job of infiltrating to the local level. This is why it is so important to look carefully at the workforce development networks that are examined in this study. They are typically not created by policy, but by grassroots efforts to provide more transparency and coordination to local labor markets. These grassroots efforts attempt to maintain some element of community control and search for ways to provide incentives for employers to participate in their programs. The goal should be to find ways to implement the Workforce Investment Act through existing community-based organizations and networks that have the local knowledge and relationships that will make this Act effective.

In the following chapters I examine employer and community college involvement in workforce development networks in rural areas. I next conduct a series of case studies to examine the organizational structure and effectiveness of these networks. The goal of this analysis is to examine how effective workforce development networks are in rural areas. Do these networks overcome the general obstacles in labor markets (such as cost, information and collective action problems), as well as the specific problems in rural areas (size and density)?

CONCLUSIONS

Rural areas face several distinct supply, demand and institutional obstacles in educating and training their workforce. On the supply side, rural areas have lower levels of human capital, workers receiving lower returns on their investments in human capital, and as a result many skilled workers migrating to urban areas. On the demand side, rural employers tend to be late in the profit or product cycle, which means they are less innovative and less likely to experience large increases in productivity. Similarly, these firms face considerable competition in their industries and are likely to experience increasingly more competition from firms overseas. Finally, because rural employers may offer low wages and fewer benefits, they may face higher turnover. High turnover rates generate a disincentive for employers to invest in job training. Institutionally, many rural areas lack intermediaries and other organizations that link workers to jobs.

The size and density of the rural population also make it difficult to develop and implement programs, especially for training. It is very costly for training institutions to offer programs to a relatively small population. Distance is an obstacle to workers and training institutions. It may be more difficult for workers to participate in training programs and for training institutions to provide programs in sparsely populated regions.

There are several limitations to traditional approaches to building local labor markets in rural areas. Traditional supply-side approaches place too much emphasis on the role of individuals and fail to consider the unique dynamics in rural labor markets. The lack of demand for skilled workers and inadequate infrastructure, such as transportation and child care, contribute to the underemployment and/or out-migration of workers with high levels of training and education. Government training programs are often heralded as the key to economic development in rural areas. They are, however, often not coordinated with local employers and linked to the real opportunities that exist in the area.

The approach to building local labor markets that is discussed in greater detail here is employer-provided training programs that are coordinated by community-based organizations and other institutions that are tied to the region. By linking together several employers, community-based approaches can reduce the cost and the disincentives to employer-provided training. Workforce development networks may offer more coordination between the supply of and demand for labor in a region.

NOTE

1. This distinction between core and periphery has been used in the economics and sociology literature to refer to different segments of industries. The core sectors are usually characterized by high levels of concentration, unionization and wages. The periphery, however, has higher levels of competition, low levels of unionization and wages.

3. Employer training: individual investments in collective goods

Research suggests that many employers in rural areas do not invest much in the formal job training of their workforce (Swaim 1995). In this chapter, I address this basic question: why do rural firms underinvest in job training? Wolfgang Streeck (1989) argues that the primary reason is the 'free labor contract'. Because workers are free to move, employers are inevitably concerned that they will not obtain a return on their investment if they provide training to workers. In this regard, skills are a collective good. Employers need a skilled workforce, but it may be irrational for individual employers to make these investments. As Streeck (1989: 94) suggests, skills are 'social production factors which capitalist firms, acting according to the rational-utilitarian model, cannot adequately generate or preserve.'

This argument does not suggest that employers will not provide any training to their workers. There will be employers that are able to provide higher wages and better benefits, and thus are able to overcome some of the collective action problems. These firms, however, probably have lower turnover rates and are able to capture the investment in their workforce. The literature does suggest, however, that firms under pressure to cut costs will most likely reduce their labor costs first by cutting back on training. The cost of training is an additional concern for many small firms.

One response to the collective action problems in employer training is for employers to invest in workplace specific training rather than the development of general skills. Again, the primary reason for investment in specific rather than general skills is because job-specific skills are less transferable to other employers in a region. If employers can create non-transferable skills, they assume they are more likely to obtain a return on their investment.

Inter-organizational and collaborative networks may help to overcome some of these obstacles (Harrison and Weiss 1998; Molina 1998). Community-based organizations, for example, may bring together several firms with common training needs (Melendez and Harrison 1998). If several firms in a region with similar training needs work together, there is less of a likelihood that individual firms will lose their investments in training. Similarly, by pooling resources, employers may be able to reduce some of their costs of training. Other strategies involve collaboration across firms in a single sector so as to improve labor market information and help firms develop skills that are in demand in these industries (Parker and Rogers 1996). Another approach is to coordinate training programs among firms within a supply chain. This approach has the advantage of providing incentives for suppliers to improve their training effort and help workers identify routes of mobility and the necessary training for these positions.

In this chapter I examine the extent of job training among a sample of firms in nonmetropolitan areas of the United States. I am interested in how much employers spend on job training, the number of workers receiving training, and the type of training received. Next, I assess the extent to which employers work with other firms (in their industry, community, and supply chain) to provide formal training programs. Finally, I examine the relationship between collaboration and level of formal training. I hypothesize that cooperation with other employers provides an incentive to employers to (a) offer formal job training to a larger percentage of their workforce; (b) make greater expenditures on formal job training; (c) provide formal training beyond on-the-job training; and (d) cooperate with other firms to provide formal job training.

THE EMPLOYER SAMPLE

I conducted a survey of 1590 firms in nonmetropolitan areas throughout the United States in 2001. The business sample was stratified by both industry (manufacturing and service industries) and the number of employees in the establishment (1–19 employees, 20–99 employees, and 100 or more employees). Approximately one-half of the sample was manufacturing establishments and the other half was service establishments. About 25 percent of the sample included small firms, 35 percent was medium-size firms, and 40 percent was large firms. The respondent for the study was the person in charge of hiring, who was the personnel manager or human resource director in most cases. Once the appropriate person was identified, only establishments that had hired workers in the past year that did not have a college degree were included.

The interviews were conducted over the telephone between January and August 2001. The interviews averaged 18 minutes. A range of 1 to 47 calls were made to obtain a complete interview, with an average of six calls per complete. The total number of completes was 1590. The overall response rate was 57.5 percent, which is considered excellent for employer surveys. The response rate was generally lower for small businesses, especially those in the service sector. For the largest establishments, the response rate was over 60 percent.

Much of the survey asked questions about employee training. See Appendix 1 for the questionnaire that was used. Because training efforts may vary considerably within the establishment for different types of positions, I chose to ask questions about the last position filled that did not require a college degree. This methodology should produce a random sample of workers (Holzer 1996).

RESEARCH ON EMPLOYER TRAINING

The literature on employer provided formal training has focused on how firm and workforce characteristics influence investments in job training. Firm characteristics such as size, industry, and internal structure, as well as workforce characteristics such as gender, race and education, make up the core of independent variables that almost all studies consider. This common empirical framework may suggest that there is an extraordinary advantage in this area, in terms of comparativeness. However, because researchers work with different data sets (National Longitudinal Survey, Survey of Employer Provided Training, and so on) or, less often, use their own, results are not always directly comparable. Some researchers have pointed to the differences in these data sets as the reason for divergent findings across studies. Some key characteristics accounting for apparently divergent findings are the relative size and industry structure of firms included in the survey, and whether the job training data were collected in reference to the last person hired, the core employees, or all employees of a firm.

There is a relative consensus in the literature about which firm characteristics are more likely to be associated with the probability of providing formal job training. Studies have consistently shown that larger businesses are much more likely to provide formal training to their workers than small establishments (Frazis *et al.* 2000; Knoke and Kalleberg 1994; Lynch and Black 1998). Lynch and Black (1998: 69) argue that this 'may be because smaller employers face higher per-unit costs in the provision of formal training due to the high initial set-up costs or that they are more concerned about losing trained employees to competitors'. Subsidiaries and branches also are more likely to provide training than are independent organizations (Knoke and Kalleberg 1994).

Formal training varies by industry. Nonmanufacturing firms are more likely to offer formal training programs than are manufacturing firms (Frazis *et al.* 1995; Frazis *et al.* 1998; Lynch and Black 1998; Veum 1995). Researchers do not agree, however, on the magnitude of these differences by industry. Formal training can vary from 'somewhat' to 'considerable' across industries. Frazis *et al.* (1995) report, for instance, that formal training varies as little as 15 percent across industries, while Lynch and Black (1988) report a variation by industry of about 40 percent. In my own interviews with manufacturing firms, I have found that service firms are much more likely to develop training programs that are less firm-specific, while manufacturing firms tend to use on-the-job training methods when they do offer it.

Another firm characteristic that influences formal job training is the organization's internal structure. David Knoke and Arne Kalleberg (1994) find that establishments with a formalized internal structure (detailed definition of workers' rights and duties in each position) and internal labor markets (promotion trajectories) are more likely to provide formal training than establishments relying on external labor markets or less formal internal structures. By directly tying training to job ladders, employers offer trained workers strong incentives to continue in the firm. This increases the likelihood of recouping their investments in human capital formation.

Some researchers have looked at how the external environment of firms influences training. Establishments facing strong product and service market competition tend to provide more training than establishments in less competitive markets (Knoke and Kalleberg 1994). Also, company-provided training is associated with the business cycle of the economy. Osterman (2001: 74) states that in tight labor markets 'employers often reduce their hiring standards and compensate by increasing the amount of training they provide.'

Findings linking employer provided formal training and workers' characteristics are much less conclusive, with the exception of employees' formal education and skills. Studies have consistently shown that more educated workers receive more training (Lynch and Black 1998; Frazis *et al.* 1998; Frazis *et al.* 2000; Swaim 1995). Workers with a bachelor's degree or higher are more likely to receive formal training than are high school graduates. This pattern of training by educational level suggests that less educated workers may become trapped in low-skill jobs as long as employers are more likely to train already more educated workers.

Evidence regarding the effects of unionization, gender and race/ethnicity on the provision of training is mixed. Frazis *et al.* (2000), for instance, find that the presence of a union at the firm reduces the probability of employer-provided formal training. This result is inconsistent with those reported by Frazis *et al.* (1995) and Knoke and Kalleberg (1994), who find a positive association between union presence and training, and with those of Lynch and Black (1998), who report no statistically significant effect of union on training.

Women tend to receive less job training from their employers than men do. Knoke and Ishio (1998: 160) indicate that controlling for various social and economic factors stipulated by theories of gender, 'the female disadvantage in the hazard rate [of entry into an initial company training program] not only failed to diminish, but actually increased substantially'. They suggest that because female employees confront higher expectations about their household and child-rearing responsibilities than their male counterparts, employers may be more likely to offer training to men. Frazis *et al.* (2000) also find that men were significantly more likely than women to obtain formal training. Veum (1995), however, does not find any gender difference in the likelihood of receiving formal training among young workers, while Frazis *et al.* (1998) found that although women reported receiving more training than men, the difference was not statistically significant at conventional levels.

Similarly mixed results are reported in the literature regarding the effects of race and ethnicity on training. Swaim (1995) report that training rates in rural areas are much lower for racial and ethnic minorities – only 25 percent of Blacks and Hispanics report any training in their job compared with 41 percent of other, mostly white, workers. Knoke and Kalleberg (1994) find that, against their expectations, the percentage of white employees in an establishment is negatively associated with the provision of training by the firm. Finally, Frazis *et al.* (1998) do not find any statistically significant effect of race on training (either formal or informal).

Human capital theory predicts that firms will be more prone to offer company-specific rather than general skills programs because employers fear they may lose their investment to another employer. Frazis *et al.* (1995), Lynch and Black (1998) and Swaim (1995) report that among those employers providing training programs, most of them are firm specific, thus confirming the theoretical expectation. The first two studies also find that larger establishments are more likely than smaller ones to offer training in general or basic skills – basic reading, writing, arithmetic or English.

Overall, the literature suggests that employer-provided training is influenced by the characteristics of firms (with firm size and industry being the major factors), internal and external structures and the characteristics of the jobs and the workforce employed in the firm. I extend this literature by also considering the relationship between collaboration among groups of employers and the provision of job training.

CHARACTERISTICS OF THE ESTABLISHMENTS

Approximately three-fourths (79 percent) of the establishments in this study were for-profit organizations (see Table 3.1 for descriptive statistics). More than one-half (53 percent) operated at more than one site. Many of

Table 3.1   Descriptive statistics

Variable	Mean	Standard Deviation
Workforce receiving training (%)	62	156
Expenditures per worker ($)	760	1770
Formal training available (1=yes)	0.59	0.49
Multi-establishment firm (1=yes)	0.53	0.50
Manufacturing firm (1=yes)	0.49	0.50
Firm size	156	331
Unskilled workers (%)	36	33
Union (%)	7	22
Women (%)	53	33
Minority (%)	19	26
Number of vacancies	4.72	17.96
Difficulty recruiting (1–4)	3.01	0.83
Market competition (1–4)	3.34	0.81
Foreign competition (1–4)	1.78	1.06
Preference for high school degree (1–3)	2.52	0.67
Preference for previous experience (1–3)	2.26	0.72
Preference for previous training (1–3)	2.05	0.76
Speak with customers (1=yes)	0.47	0.50
Reading/writing reports (1=yes)	0.46	0.50
Arithmetic (1=yes)	0.51	0.50
Personal computer (1=yes)	0.30	0.46
Chances for promotion (0–4)	2.72	1.22
Cooperate with firms in industry (1=yes)	0.40	0.49
Cooperate with firms in community (1=yes)	0.35	0.48
Cooperate with firms in supply chain (1=yes)	0.29	0.46

Source: National Survey of Employer Training in Rural America (2001).

the establishments have been operating at their sites for a long time. About one-third (37 percent) began operating in their current site before 1970. Approximately 20 percent began operating during each of the three following decades – 1970s, 1980s and 1990s.

The average establishment had 156 employees (including permanent full- and part-time workers and temporary or seasonal employees), with the range between 1 and 5700. The median was 60 employees. The average workforce was nonunion, with only about 10 percent of the establishments having any current employees covered by a collective bargaining agreement.

Approximately one-half of the average workforce in these organizations was female and about 20 percent was of a minority ethnic or racial background.

Approximately three-fourths of the establishments had jobs that did not require any particular skills, education, previous training, or experience when workers were hired. Among those establishments not requiring those skills, training or experience, about one-half of them said those employees did not perform any significant reading, writing or arithmetic on the job. It should be pointed out again that the screening process selected only employers that had recently hired someone without a college degree. This would mean that employers requiring more educated employers would be less likely to be included in the sample.

Most employers reported they were facing some difficulty hiring qualified applicants at the time of the survey. This survey was conducted at the top of a business cycle when demand was only just beginning to slow down. Prior to this time, most regions had been experiencing a labor shortage. Only about one-fourth (23 percent) reported that hiring was easy, while 47 percent said that it was somewhat difficult and 30 percent indicated it was very difficult.

The literature suggests that the level of domestic and foreign competition may influence how much employers are willing to invest in job training. I asked employers how much domestic competition their firms faced in their main markets or service areas. The majority (52 percent) answered that they faced a great deal of competition, about one-third (34 percent) some, 11 percent a little and 4 percent no competition. Foreign competition, however, was remarkably less important for most employers. The majority (59 percent) said their organization faced no foreign competition, 15 percent a little, 15 percent some and only 11 percent of employers maintained that they faced a great deal of foreign competition. This finding is a bit surprising as it is often assumed that firms in rural areas are now in markets that are global in scale. It suggests that most employers operate primarily in regional markets.

TRAINING EFFORT

Most establishments devoted some organizational resources toward job training over the past two years. Only about one-half of the establishments reported any training expenditures during this period. Among those establishments that have invested resources in job training, the average amount was $50 000 for the 2000–2001 period (median = $10 000). As can be seen from Figure 3.1, most firms spent a relatively small

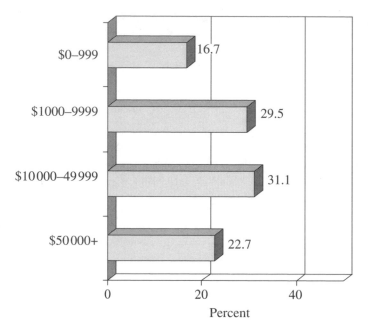

Source: National Survey of Employer Training in Rural America (2001).

Figure 3.1   Amount of money spent on job training in 2000–2001

amount of formal job training over 2000–2001. An average of 85 (median = 15) workers have participated in formal training programs, which was just over one-half their workforce.

As discussed above, most studies have found that firm size is strongly related to training effort. Large firms spend considerably more than small firms do on formal training (Figure 3.2). When I calculate the per capita expenditures, small firms face a much larger burden (Figure 3.3). Small firms spend more than twice as much per capita as large firms do on formal training. These findings clearly explain some of the reasons for the training gap between small and large firms.

How do employers provide training? Almost all (94 percent) of the establishments that provided training offered in-house (on-site) programs. Approximately one-half (55 percent) provided in-house training programs by company staff (Figure 3.4). Thirty percent of employers used community-based organizations to provide in-house programs. Far fewer establishments offered off-site training at corporate headquarters or at an educational institution. Among those firms that contracted off-site training with external agencies, were those firms most likely to employ the

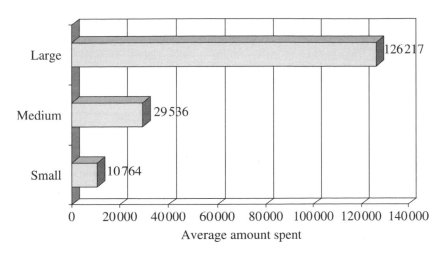

Source: National Survey of Employer Training in Rural America (2001).

Figure 3.2   Firm size and amount of money spent on job training in 2000–2001

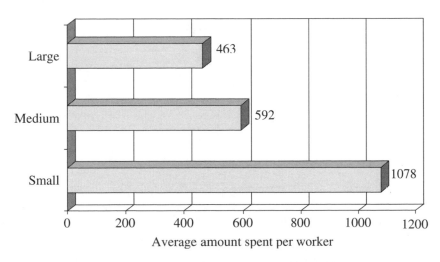

Source: National Survey of Employer Training in Rural America (2001).

Figure 3.3   Firm size and amount of money spent on job training per worker in 2000–2001

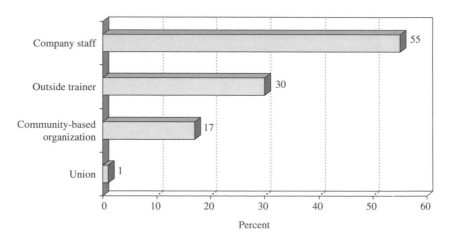

Source: National Survey of Employer Training in Rural America (2001).

Figure 3.4   How training is provided in-house

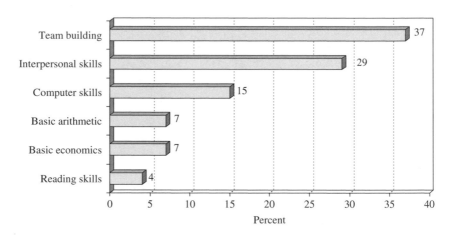

Source: National Survey of Employer Training in Rural America (2001).

Figure 3.5   Types of training provided for position that did not require a college degree

services of an educational institution (56 percent of the cases) or a community-based organization (28 percent of the cases).

What types of training did employers provide? Employers were most likely to provide training on group or team building (Figure 3.5). Approximately

37 percent of those establishments offering training had group/team building programs. About one-third (29 percent) offered training programs in interpersonal skills, and 15 percent provided training in computer skills, such as word processing or data management; 7 percent in basic arithmetic or math; 7 percent provided training in basic economics; and 4 percent in improving reading skills. So, it does not appear that many employers provide training in basic skills. They do offer training programs for 'soft' skills, but rarely provide the type of general computer or math skills that would lead to higher level skills and earnings. Of course, there are several ways to interpret these data. It may be the case that employers perceive that the level of math or computer skills is adequate for the types of jobs available in the firm. Another possible interpretation is that employers still do not believe the workforce has adequate math or computer skills, but they believe it is the worker's responsibility to obtain these skills and the employers are unwilling to pay for it.

Among those employers providing training, I asked whether the amount of training for the last person hired had increased, decreased, or remained about the same over the past three years. Almost none of the employers reported that the amount of training had decreased. About one-half said that it had increased, while the other half said that it had stayed about the same. The most common reasons for increasing the amount of training were concern about the quality of work and adoption of new management practices. Lastly, employers were asked if they anticipated that the amount of training for the position was going to increase; 47 percent said that it would increase; 53 percent thought it would stay the same; and only 1 percent thought it would decrease.

JOB-RELATED CHARACTERISTICS OF LAST PERSON HIRED

One of the difficulties in studying employer training is that firms may offer training to some employees, but not others. One strategy for dealing with this problem is to collect information on the same type of employee across firms. I took the approach of asking questions about the last person hired for a position that did not require a college degree. This strategy provides a random sample of jobs that are unskilled or semi-skilled. Thus, it should be kept in mind that the results did not include positions that required a college or professional degree.

I first asked to what extent it was preferred that the person had a high school diploma (Figure 3.6). Many employers use a high school diploma as an important signal of the future productivity of the worker: 63 percent

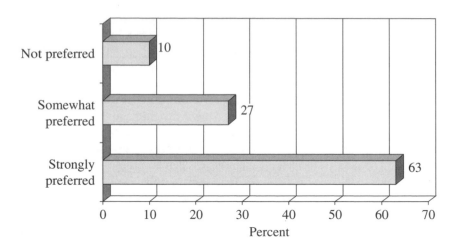

Source: National Survey of Employer Training in Rural America (2001).

Figure 3.6   High school degree requirement

said it was strongly preferred, 27 percent indicated that it was somewhat preferred, and only 10 percent suggested it was not at all preferred. It should be noted that this preference may change with labor market conditions. In times of high unemployment, employers can be more selective and they may be more likely to require a high school diploma under these conditions. Given the labor market situation when these data were collected, however, it is likely that employers were much less selective regarding this issue.

Next, I queried employers about how important it was for a person to have had previous experience in that specific line of work (Figure 3.7). Forty-two percent of employers indicated that it was strongly preferred and the same number said it was somewhat preferred. The rest indicated that it was not preferred at all. Finally, I asked to what extent having general previous training or certification was preferred (Figure 3.8). Employers were less concerned with this last issue. About one-third (27 percent) of them said it was not preferred at all, 42 percent indicated it was somewhat preferred, and less than one-third (31 percent) said it was strongly preferred.

The types of tasks involved in the position occupied by the last person hired over the last year may influence their level of training (Figure 3.9). Almost one-half (47 percent) of employers said the position involved speaking directly with customers in person or over the phone; 46 percent indicated that it involved reading or writing reports, memos or lengthy instructions; 51 percent mentioned it involved doing arithmetic, including

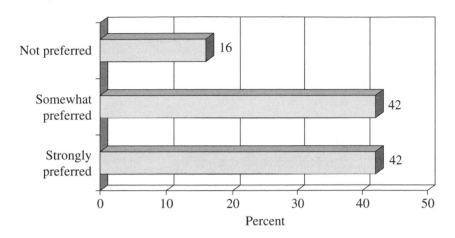

Source: National Survey of Employer Training in Rural America (2001).

Figure 3.7   Previous experience

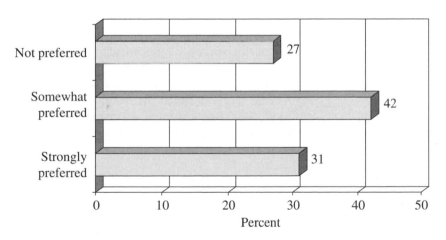

Source: National Survey of Employer Training in Rural America (2001).

Figure 3.8   Previous training or skill certification

making change; and 30 percent said it included using a personal computer. All these activities were required on a daily basis.

I also asked questions about the chances of promotion and the time it typically takes for someone hired for a position that did not require a college degree to be promoted. About a third (31 percent) of employers said

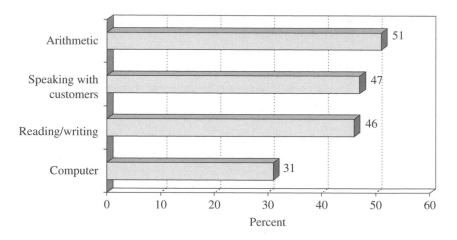

Source: National Survey of Employer Training in Rural America (2001).

Figure 3.9   Employees' daily tasks

that if the person performed well, the chances to be promoted were excellent, a similar proportion (35 percent) indicated that they were good, 17 percent thought that they were fair, and only 9 percent said the chances to be promoted were poor. Most employers (60 percent) indicated that a person hired for a non-college degree position had to wait years to obtain a promotion. The rest of employers considered that it typically takes less than a year: 33 percent indicated it takes months, 1 percent said it takes weeks, and 6 percent maintained it takes days to be promoted.

COORDINATION WITH OTHER EMPLOYERS

I next assessed whether and how employers coordinate their training efforts with other firms in their industry and region (Figure 3.10). Forty-four percent of the employers collaborated with other firms in the same industry to identify common skills required for workers that were in comparable jobs. Thirty-eight percent said they collaborated with firms of the same community and 26 percent did so with firms in their supply chain. I also asked employers whether they cooperated with other firms in developing training programs aimed at increasing or improving their workers' skills. Forty percent developed programs with firms that are in the same industry, 35 percent did that with firms of the same community and 29 percent did so with firms in their supply chain.

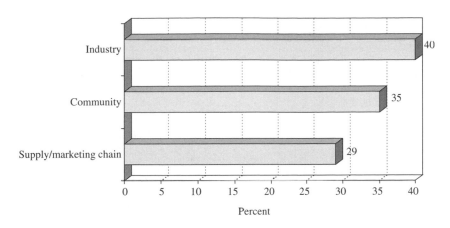

Source: National Survey of Employer Training in Rural America (2001).

Figure 3.10   Work with other companies to develop training programs

Nineteen percent of the employers requested community organizations to develop and provide training programs. About the same number of employers (21 percent) worked with community-based organizations to recruit workers. A smaller proportion of employers (11 percent) collaborated with community-based organizations in pre-employment programs for potential workers. These programs are usually directed at workers who have weak work histories or need some basic skills related to job interviews, punctuality and other soft skills. Lastly, two-fifths (42 percent) of employers were involved in training programs with local high schools, such as the school-to-work programs, while only one-third of them offered apprenticeship programs.

Manufacturing and service industries differed substantially in their willingness to collaborate with community-based organizations. Service industry firms were about twice as likely as manufacturing firms to collaborate with community-based organizations in providing training programs and worker recruitment services. I believe one of the main reasons for this difference is that service firms find it easier to identify common skill needs than do manufacturing firms. For example, commercial banks have a similar set of occupations and training needs that can be addressed. Manufacturing firms tend to have more specialized needs and are less likely to have a common set of training needs in a region. There also may be more competition within the manufacturing sector compared to the services sector.

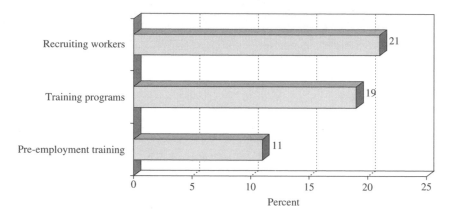

Source: National Survey of Employer Training in Rural America (2001).

Figure 3.11 Work with community organizations over the last two years

Manufacturing and service firms also differed in their willingness to offer school-to-work and apprenticeship programs. About one-half (47 percent) of service firms offered school-to work programs, while 37 percent of manufacturing firms offered them. Thirty-seven percent of service firms offered apprenticeship programs, compared to 28 percent of manufacturing firms. I will discuss some of the dilemmas in school-to-work and apprenticeship programs in the next chapter. One of the key issues is the need to offer educational and training programs at a sufficient scale. It is probably the case that service firms have more general needs that can be met through these programs. Another factor in rural areas, however, is the lack of unions. In urban areas, unions play a critical role in establishing and maintaining apprenticeship programs, especially among manufacturers. Without unions, it is much more difficult to develop these formal programs.

I examined other factors that influence the use of job training services offered by community-based organizations (Figure 3.11). Employer characteristics such as size, skill level and the number of vacant positions affected the likelihood of collaboration with community-based organizations. Firms that used community-based organizations for job training were approximately twice as large on average and had twice as many unskilled positions. The gender and racial composition of firms in the service industry also influenced the likelihood of working with community-based organizations. Service firms comprised of a larger percentage of females and minority employees and were more likely to cooperate with

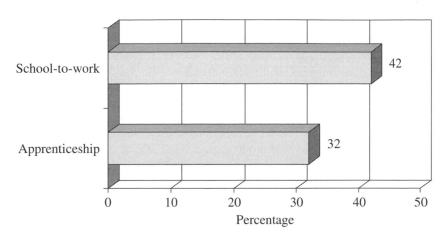

Source: National Survey of Employer Training in Rural America (2001).

Figure 3.12 Employer program involvement

community-based organizations. It is difficult to establish with these data whether cooperation led them to hire more minorities, or the reverse.

Several employer characteristics affected collaboration with community-based organizations to recruit workers. For manufacturing and service industries, large firms with many unskilled positions were more likely to use these organizations to recruit workers. The gender composition of the workforce was a factor for the manufacturing industry. Manufacturing firms that collaborated with community-based organizations to recruit workers had more female employees. Service industry firms that utilized community-based organizations to recruit workers averaged twice as many vacancies as those that did not utilize them.

I looked at employer involvement in school-to-work and apprenticeship programs (Figure 3.12). Large firms with a higher percentage of female employees were more likely to be involved with these programs. Manufacturing firms with a higher percentage of minority employees were less likely to be involved with them. However, this did not influence service firms. Manufacturing and service firms in the Midwest were most likely to be involved with school-to-work programs. Involvement of manufacturing firms facing more foreign competition was also higher. Foreign competition in the service industry did not influence their involvement in school-to-work programs.

Several factors influenced employers offering apprenticeship programs. Both manufacturing and service firms offering apprenticeships averaged about twice the size of firms not offering them. Vacancies and unionization for service industry firms was also a factor. Service firms offering apprenticeships averaged twice as many vacancies and had a higher percentage of unionized employees. Manufacturing industry employers were more likely to offer apprenticeships if they faced higher foreign competition, while service firms were not.

Manufacturing firms in nonmetropolitan areas with populations above 20 000 were more likely to offer apprenticeship programs compared to firms in more rural areas. As one might expect, firm size is strongly related to employer involvement in school-to-work and apprenticeship programs. Large firms have more demand for apprenticeships and have more resources to invest in these programs. As I will discuss in the next chapter, I believe this is largely due to the scale that is required for these programs. Large communities and firms can more easily develop apprenticeship and school-to-work programs.

MULTIVARIATE ANALYSES OF TRAINING EFFORT

To examine the central hypothesis that cooperation with other employers provides an incentive for a firm to offer formal job training to a larger percentage of their workforce and to make greater expenditures on formal job training, I conducted a two-stage least square regression analysis of training effort on several firm characteristics. Only the results from the second stage are reported here. The two-stage regression model was used in this analysis because of the simultaneity between collaboration and job training. In other words, collaboration may increase training expenditures which increases the incentive to cooperate even more as a way to lower costs. The two-stage regression model is the most appropriate technique to handle this problem. The goal was to assess whether coordinating efforts have an effect over and above firms' characteristics that influence training effort. In Table 3.2, I report the results of the two-stage regression analysis of the percentage of the workforce that has received formal training in the last two years.

Key firm characteristics (firm size, industry, skill level of the workforce and branch plant status) have strong effects on the percentage of the workforce that receives formal training. Large and service firms provide formal training to a larger percentage of their workforce than do small and manufacturing firms. Although the relationships are weaker, multi-establishment firms and establishments with a higher percentage of skilled workers also tend to provide formal training to a larger percentage of their workforce than independent establishments and firms with a larger percentage of unskilled

Table 3.2   Two-stage ordinary least squares regression analysis of percentage of workforce receiving formal training (log)

Multi-establishment firm (1=yes)	0.361*** (0.110)	0.373*** (0.114)	0.383*** (0.116)
Manufacturing firm (1=yes)	−0.563*** (−0.172)	−0.631*** (−0.192)	−0.639*** (−0.194)
Firm size (log)	0.205*** (0.191)	0.190*** (0.177)	0.207*** (0.192)
Unskilled workers (%)	−0.391** (−0.079)	−0.368** (−0.074)	−0.418** (−0.084)
Difficulty recruiting	0.133** (0.066)	0.153** (0.077)	0.152** (0.076)
Cooperate with firms in industry	0.564*** (0.168)		
Cooperate with firms in community		0.576*** (0.167)	
Cooperate with firms in marketing/supply chain			0.500*** (0.138)
Constant	−2.567***	−2.524***	−2.526***
F	40.557***	41.661***	38.148***
R-square	0.150	0.149	0.142
N	1385	1388	1384

**p < 0.01$; ***p < 0.001$.

Note: Standardized regression coefficients (betas) are in parentheses.

Source: From 'Collaborative job training in rural America,' by Gary Paul Green, Valeia Galetto and Anna Haines, 2003. Reprinted by permission of the *Journal of Research in Rural Education* 18(2): 78–85 (http://www.acclaim-math.org/docs/jrre_archives/v18,n2, p 78-85,Green,Galetto,Haines.pdf).

workers. Also, as expected, employers experiencing greater difficulty hiring qualified workers train more of their workforce. Employers see these investments as a way to retain their workers in a tight labor market situation.

Finally, I assessed whether collaborative training programs are correlated with the percentage of the workforce that is formally trained, while controlling for other firm characteristics. Collaboration with firms in their industry, community and marketing/supply chain all are positively related to formal training, and the effects are robust. Cooperation with firms in their industry and community has stronger effects than cooperation with firms in the marketing/supply chain. Looking at the standardized beta coefficients (presented in the parentheses), coordination with firms in the same industry or community has the strongest effects in the model, with the exception of firm size.

These findings lend strong support for the argument that encouraging cooperation among employers will lead to higher levels of formal training in the workplace. The strength of the relationships is especially impressive. Along with firm size, collaboration is strongly related to training effort. It was somewhat surprising to find that collaboration across industry and community is about equally important. I will explore this issue more in the next two chapters. There are good reasons, however, to believe that there may be qualitative differences in the types of training available in these different types of collaborations.

Table 3.3   Two-stage ordinary least squares regression analysis of expenditures on formal training per worker (log)

Multi-establishment firm (1=yes)	0.419 (0.060)	0.419 (0.060)	0.439 (0.063)
Manufacturing firm (1=yes)	0.137 (0.019)	0.137 (0.020)	0.131 (0.019)
Firm size (log)	0.390*** (0.172)	0.399*** (0.172)	0.401*** (0.177)
Unskilled workers (%)	−0.610 (−0.057)	−0.610 (−0.057)	−0.587 (−0.055)
Difficulty recruiting	0.584*** (0.143)	0.584*** (0.143)	0.593*** (0.146)
Cooperate with firms in industry	0.638*** (0.087)		
Cooperate with firms in community		0.637* (0.087)	
Cooperate with firms in marketing/supply chain			0.841** (0.109)
Constant	1.141*	1.141*	1.041*
F	10.166***	10.166**	10.845***
R-square	0.072	0.072	0.076
N	797	797	797

*$p<0.05$; **$p<0.01$; ***$p<0.001$.

Note: Standardized regression coefficients (betas) are in parentheses.

Source: From 'Collaborative job training in rural America,' by Gary Paul Green, Valeria Galetto and Anna Haines, 2003. Reprinted by permission of the *Journal of Research in Rural Education* 18(2): 78–85 (http://www.acclaim-math.org/docs/jrre_archives/v18,n2, p 78-85,Green,Galetto,Haines.pdf).

I next examined the effects of collaboration on expenditures for formal training per worker, while controlling for other firm characteristics (Figure 3.3). The relationships between cooperation with firms are significant for all three types of cooperation: industry, community and marketing/supply chain. The effects are generally not as strong the firm characteristics, such as firm size. Collaboration provides incentives to train more workers but it does not affect the resources devoted to training. The resource issue seems to be driven by firm size more than anything else.

In the next step of the analysis, I examined the factors influencing training effort at the individual level by determining the likelihood that an employer provides formal training, beyond on-the-job training, to the last person hired in the firm (Table 3.4). The independent variables in this analysis are essentially the same (firm characteristics and firm linkages), except that it also includes several variables measuring job characteristics. I include the qualifications required for the job and the specific responsibilities required for the position. Finally, I include the opportunities for advancement. All of these variables should have an effect on the likelihood that a worker would receive formal training. This type of analysis has both advantages and disadvantages. The advantage is that we can control for the actual skills and requirements of the jobs, which may dictate how much training occurs. The disadvantage is that this analysis will tell us less about the organizational commitment to formal training because we are analyzing training effort at the individual level.

Overall, many of the firm's characteristics operate in different directions than they did in the firm-level analysis. Workers in large firms are more likely to receive formal training. The exception is that branch plant status operates in a different direction once the job characteristics are controlled for in the analysis. Manufacturing firms also are more likely than service firms to provide job training. Difficulty recruiting is not statistically related to formal training in this analysis. Preference for a high school degree is strongly related to the likelihood that a worker receives formal training. The only other job characteristic that is strongly related to the likelihood of receiving formal job training is whether the worker is required to read and write reports on a daily basis. This variable, however, is negatively related to the likelihood that the worker received formal training. Opportunity for promotion also is strongly related to the likelihood of receiving formal training. This analysis does suggest that job requirements do help explain some of the differences across firms in their commitment to formal job training.

In the next analysis, I use logistic regression to estimate the likelihood that a firm cooperates with other firms to develop formal training programs (Table 3.5). Overall, the model appears to be much stronger for cooperation with firms in the industry and community than with firms in the supply

Workforce development networks in rural areas

Table 3.4   Logistic regression analysis of likelihood that employer provides formal training beyond on-the-job training

Firm characteristics			
Multi-establishment firm	−0.267*	−0.244*	−0.281
Manufacturing firm	0.656***	0.704***	0.713***
Firm size (log)	0.202***	0.195***	0.215***
Unskilled workers (%)	−0.215	−0.191	−0.243
Union (%)	0.001	0.001	0.000
Women (%)	0.000	0.000	0.000
Minority (%)	−0.004	−0.004	−0.003
Number of vacancies	−0.014*	−0.014*	−0.013*
Difficulty recruiting	0.029	0.051	0.050
Market competition	−0.034	−0.044	−0.050
Foreign competition	0.054	0.042	0.042
Job characteristics			
High school degree preferred	0.309**	0.268**	0.295**
Previous experience preferred	0.136	0.146	0.158
Previous training provided	0.128	0.122	0.130
Speak directly with customers	0.134	0.144	0.105
Read/write reports	−0.401**	−0.443***	−0.428***
Use arithmetic	−0.150	−0.154	−0.150
Use computer	−0.121	−0.109	−0.108
Chances for promotion	0.171***	0.180***	0.183***
Firm linkages			
Cooperate with firms in industry	−0.602***		
Cooperate with firms in community		−0.663***	
Cooperate with firms in marketing/supply chain			−0.414**
Constant	−1.899***	−1.741**	−2.081***
Log likelihood	1536.486	1533.528	1545.250
Degrees of freedom	20	20	20
Cox & Snell *R* Square	0.125	0.129	0.119
N	1252	1255	1252

*p<0.05; **p<0.01; ***p<0.001.

Source: National Survey of Employer Training in Rural America (2001).

Table 3.5   *Logistic regression analysis of likelihood that employer cooperates with other firms to provide formal training programs*

	Industry	Community	Supply/marketing Chain
Multi-establishment firm	−0.251*	−0.337**	−0.172
Manufacturing firm	0.727***	0.478*	0.517*
Firm size (log)	0.136**	0.264***	0.121**
Unskilled workers (%)	−0.454**	−0.845***	−0.223
Union (%)	0.003	0.000	0.004
Women (%)	0.003	0.001	0.004
Minority (%)	0.004	0.006*	0.000
Number of vacancies	0.008	0.011	−0.002
Difficulty recruiting	0.104	0.036	0.000
Market competition	0.024	0.033	0.209
Foreign competition	−0.054	0.087	0.109
Constant	−1.866***	−2.383***	−2.758***
Log likelihood	1614.813	1534.331	1494.007
Degrees of freedom	11	11	11
Cox & Snell *R*-Square	0.077	0.085	0.036
N	1277	1280	1277

*p<0.05; **p<0.01; ***p<0.001.

Source: National Survey of Employer Training in Rural America (2001).

chain. The strongest effects in the model are for the skill level of the firm, industry, firm size, and branch plant status. Firms most likely to be engaged in cooperation with other firms to develop training programs are large firms, those with few unskilled workers, manufacturing firms, and independent firms.

In addition to participation in these consortiums, employers work with community-based organizations devoted to workforce development issues. CBOs can play a variety of roles, such as intermediaries that provide support services and linkages to other organizations and institutions (Fitzgerald 1998). Two-fifths (42 percent) of employers were involved in training programs with local high schools, such as school-to-work programs, while only one-third of them offered apprenticeship programs.

I then estimated a model for employer collaboration with CBOs. Two employer characteristics are strongly related to the use of CBOs for training, recruiting and pre-employment training: firm size and industrial sector (Table 3.6). Large firms are much more likely to collaborate with CBOs in

*Table 3.6   Logistic regression analysis of likelihood that employers
               collaborate with community-based organizations*

	Training	Recruitment	Pre-employment training
Firm size (log)	0.385***	0.346***	0.232***
Manufacturing sector	−0.503**	−0.554***	−0.492**
Work cooperatively (1–4)	−0.471**	0.231*	−0.441**
Workers not required to read/write (%)	−0.531*		
Workers not receiving formal training (%)	0.253***		
Vacancies (%)		0.178**	0.171*
Constant	−1.638***	−1.479***	−1.512***
Log likelihood	911.435	1468.915	1015.295
Degrees of freedom	5	4	4
Cox & Snell *R* Square	0.098	0.070	0.033
N	1043	1522	1530

*p<0.05; ** p<0.01; *** p<0.001.

Source: National Survey of Employer Training in Rural America (2001).

these activities. Large firms recruit more workers and thus have greater
needs for training and related services. Also, working with CBOs may take
time and other resources that are less available to small firms.

Service firms are much more likely to collaborate with CBOs than are
manufacturing firms. Manufacturing firms often report that their training
needs are so unique that they see few benefits in participating in these collaborative efforts. Similarly, their training needs may be met more often by
on-site (on-the-job) programs rather than off-site.

There are a few additional factors influencing employers' likelihood
of collaborating with CBOs. As one might expect, employers with a
higher percentage of positions not requiring reading or writing are less
likely to work with a CBO to provide training. With less demand for skilled
workers, employers do not perceive as many advantages to participation in
these collaborative efforts. Similarly, employers with a larger percentage of
their workforce receiving formal training are more likely to collaborate
with CBOs.

The vacancy rate (number of vacancies/number of full-time employees)
is strongly correlated with the likelihood that employers work with
CBOs to recruit workers and to provide pre-employment training. I interpret this finding to suggest that labor shortages can be a strong motivator

to participate in workforce development networks as a strategy to recruit qualified workers. This finding is corroborated in the case studies. The labor shortage encouraged employers to collaborate with CBOs, community colleges and government agencies. Most firms are willing to go beyond their usual recruiting strategies to find qualified workers in these situations.

CONCLUSIONS

The survey of employers in the nonmetropolitan areas of the US reveals that job training and productivity are becoming increasingly important. Although most employers report that it is competition that is pushing them to become more productive, relatively few of the employers report that it is foreign competition that is producing the changes in the workplace. It may be the case that almost all rural service firms, and most rural manufacturing firms, serve regional markets that are not as exposed to international competition.

As expected, I found relatively low levels of formal training among employers. Only about 50 percent of the average workforce is receiving any formal training and almost one-fourth of the positions in the average workforce do not require that the worker perform reading, writing or arithmetic on the job. Some of the evidence suggests that the skills required for these jobs is increasing, but there is still a large proportion of the workforce in jobs requiring very little education or training.

I did find that a surprisingly large number of firms are cooperating with each other to develop training programs. Employers are most likely to work with firms in their own industry or their community to identify common skill needs or to develop new training programs. Participation in these networks tends to encourage employers to make a greater effort to train their workforce. I also found that many nonmetropolitan employers are working with community-based organizations to provide pre-employment training, job matching, and even job training programs.

The most important point to take away from this analysis is that collaboration does appear to provide strong incentives for employers to invest in their workforce. One of the key obstacles to improved training is the collection action problem I discussed in the previous chapter. Most employers are unwilling to provide formal training because they fear they may lose their investments to other employers. Although I have provided some evidence that collaboration can improve the training effort by employers, it is difficult to assess how broad the training is with this type of analysis. In the following chapters I will explore in more detail how the form and structure of collaboration between employers and other organizations may influence the breadth of training offered to their workforce.

In the next chapter I examine the role of community colleges in workforce development networks. I examine several related questions. How often do they participate in these collaborations among employers? What do they see as the benefits and costs of collaboration? And, does collaboration change the type of training programs they offer? I will extend this analysis of employer collaboration by analyzing how community colleges initiate, intervene and respond to these efforts.

4. Community colleges in rural America: new roles and challenges

Over the past few decades, community colleges across rural America have become more engaged in regional economic development. Globalization and technological change have contributed to job losses in many rural areas. Some regions have experienced population and job growth, but many of these areas have become dependent on tourism and retail industries that provide low wages, no benefits and few opportunities for mobility. Technological change has increased the need for rural areas to develop a skilled and trained workforce to compete in a global economy in the twenty-first century.

Community colleges were created to provide the first two years of a four-year college education. Their original focus was, therefore, on what was known as the transfer function. Students who completed two years of undergraduate education and earned an associate's degree at a two-year college could transfer to a four-year college to complete a bachelor's degree. Over time, however, community colleges widened their initial mission. There are several reasons for this shift. Community colleges often rely heavily on local taxes for funding. By promoting development they hope to increase the tax base as well as garner public support in the region. Community colleges that focus on the transfer function also open themselves up to the criticism that they are elitist institutions that fail to address the educational needs of the working class. Regional economic development activities push community colleges to address the educational needs of a much different population.

Autry and Rubin (1998: 3) assert that rural community colleges are uniquely positioned as catalysts for economic development. They are 'common ground' institutions and thus 'can be a safe, neutral place for mobilizing community engagement and building social capital'. The authors suggest that community colleges may contribute to the economic development of their service areas in the following ways:

1. Provide regional leadership. Community colleges can bring together representatives from a broad cross-section of the community to build an economic development agenda and engage them to carry it out.

2. Promote technology transfer and small business development. Community colleges can promote the transfer of technology by organizing manufacturing networks and serving as brokers between area businesses and specialized technical assistance sources.
3. Offer workforce development programs that are responsive to employers' changing needs. Community colleges can deliver a wide array of services designed to meet individual employers' education and training needs. These range from soft-skills training for entry-level positions to workshops on quality standards for managerial positions.

Although there are unique opportunities for community colleges to contribute to regional economic development, there are also concerns. Some critics charge that community colleges have become too responsive to employer needs and fail to provide the general training that will help workers become upwardly mobile (Rogers *et al.* 1990). Another way of putting this is to say that community colleges are responding to private rather than public needs. The rise of workforce development networks, however, may enable community colleges to realize their promise in regional economic development. These networks may assist in achieving simultaneously the goals of responding to employer needs and providing basic skills to the workforce that will improve their productivity and their opportunities for advancement.

In this chapter I look at the evolving mission of rural community colleges and their role in workforce development networks. I focus more on the direct economic development mission of community colleges than their transfer function. More specifically, I am interested in the following questions: How do community colleges work with community-based organizations, employers and other institutions to deliver workforce development programs? What are some of the conflicts and contradictions between the missions of the transfer function and regional economic development? How do community colleges initiate workforce development efforts? Why do they do it?

I begin with a discussion of contract training. Part of the regional economic development mission of community colleges is developing specific training programs for employers. I discuss the extent to which community colleges are involved in these activities and who the primary beneficiaries are.

CONTRACT TRAINING

Contract training programs are classes offered to employees of business and industry. Typically this type of training is very specialized and is developed in collaboration with employers. The number of contract training programs offered by community colleges has grown rapidly since the 1980s. A survey of 16 of the nation's leading community college systems reports that while in 1980–1 they offered 132 programs in contract training, in 1987–8 they offered 1700 (Kent 1991: 32). Likewise, Kane and Rouse (1999) find that at the end of the 1980s, 94 percent of community colleges offered at least one contract training course to business and industry, and that the median ratio of contract to regular credit enrollment in the 1988–9 academic year was 0.22 (about one contract student for every five regular ones). A recent study by the US Government Accountability Office (2004) found that most of the contract training was provided in fields that are projected to be high growth areas in the next few decades – health care, business and information technology.

Contract training supply, however, is unevenly distributed among community colleges. In fact, in a recent publication Dougherty (2003: 85) finds that 'while most community colleges offer contract training, some offer a lot and many only a little'. This variation among community colleges may be due, according to Dougherty, to the magnitude of local employer demand for contract training, the degree of leadership and commitment of community college administrators to contribute to the economic development of the community at large, and the amount of financial and human resources devoted to design new curricula that is responsive to employers' needs, to equip and maintain up-to-date facilities, and to hire appropriate instructors or adequately train community college staff.

Although all factors are important, there is consensus in the literature that financial and human resources are crucial in determining a community college's capacity to offer a large, diverse and meaningful supply of contract training programs to employers (Brint 2003; Fitzgerald 1998; Rubin and Autry 1998). Fitzgerald, for instance, examines the characteristics of community colleges that succeeded in reaching out to the business community and finds that staff allocation and adequate funding are essential to the development of effective business outreach programs (Fitzgerald 1998). The lack of financial and human resources is undoubtedly a major obstacle for rural community colleges.

Contract Training Beneficiaries

What types of firms are more likely to rely on community colleges to provide contract training? Business use of community colleges varies greatly across firm size and industry. Larger firms enroll their employees in contract training programs more often than do smaller firms. Dougherty (2003: 83) argues that the disproportionate use of employee training by large businesses is best explained 'in terms of the magnitude of their provision of formal training to employees and in their willingness to use community colleges to provide that training'. Large establishments provide more formal training because, among other things, they are more capital intensive, have more developed job structures and internal labor markets, and have a greater capacity to absorb training costs including the cost of losing a trained worker to a competitor (Dougherty 2003).

Manufacturing, health care, transportation, communication, utility and finance and insurance firms work with community colleges much more frequently than do wholesale and retail trade, apparel making and construction firms. Some factors that may account for this different industry usage are related to the average size of business establishments (and their concomitant higher propensity to provide formal training), state subsidies for employee training that are biased toward certain industries, and community colleges' preferences for working with certain industries rather than others (Dougherty 2003).

The objective of this chapter is to examine the roles of community colleges in rural areas in providing job training and delivering services to regional businesses. I am especially interested in how they are balancing customized training programs versus traditional class room instruction, why they were involved in collaborative efforts to deliver training, and what the demand for business services was in their region. I conducted a survey of approximately 250 community colleges that are delivering training programs in rural America. Although these institutions use a variety of names today, I will use the term 'community college' in this chapter.

THE COMMUNITY COLLEGE SAMPLE

The sample of rural community colleges for this survey was drawn from the national survey of nonmetropolitan firms reported in the previous chapter. In that survey I asked respondents to identify the community/technical college that provided them with the majority of services in their region. Because I used a random sample of employers, this procedure should yield a random sample of community colleges in nonmetropolitan America. This strategy produced 338 community colleges identified by the employer survey. I obtained the full address, telephone number and name of a contact person at each institution through the internet. The University of Wisconsin Survey Center conducted a screening call at each institution to obtain up-to-date address and contact information, as well as give advance notice that they would be receiving a survey. Many community colleges have several different branches. In these instances I chose to identify the closest campus to the firm if the specific branch was not mentioned by the employer. Appendix 2 provides a copy of the questionnaire used in this stage of the study.

Data collection involved two stages: a mail survey and telephone interview. The design for the mail survey called for a full mailing to respondents (including a cover letter, survey, and business reply envelope), a postcard reminder to all respondents, and then a reminder mailing to those respondents who had not yet returned their survey. After the reminder mailing was sent, the Survey Center conducted a round of personal touch calls to non-respondents. The mail survey generated 97 completes. Six weeks after the last mailing was sent, the Survey Center began calling non-respondents to conduct the survey over the telephone. A total of 149 interviews were completed in this manner, for a total of 246 completed surveys. The overall response rate was 74 percent. I asked questions about academic programs, faculty and staff, training needs of the region, apprenticeship programs, services, collaboration and involvement in economic development activities in the region.

Given the sample design used in the study, it would be impossible to assess how representative these community colleges are. The fact that the employer survey only included rural employers that had recently hired a worker not requiring a college degree means that the sample of community colleges cannot be considered representative of all community colleges in the US. When we look at the location of the community colleges in the study, we find that most are located in either the Midwest or South (Figure 4.1). Also, most of these community colleges are located in the smaller counties, but not in the very smallest (Figure 4.2). The low population size and density in these very small counties may make it difficult to support a community college.

The Institutions

Rural community colleges tend to be smaller and serve broader areas than do urban community colleges. In Table 4.1, I report the enrollment and finances of community colleges in urban and rural areas of the US. As can be seen, relatively few community colleges are located in rural areas, but a significant number are in small towns. Rural community colleges tend to have smaller enrollments than urban ones. Also the revenue per student is much higher in rural and small town areas than in metropolitan areas.

I collected some basic information on the size and breadth of the programs offered in rural community colleges during the 2000–1 academic year.[1] The average community college in the sample has about 75 full-time faculty and 123 part-time faculty on campus. Approximately 1600 full-time and 3400 part-time students were enrolled at these institutions during this time period. The community colleges reported that about 350 students, on

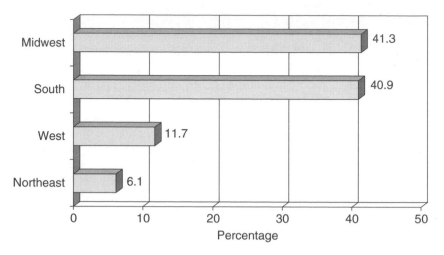

Source: National Survey of Rural Community Colleges (2002).

Figure 4.1   Community colleges in census regions

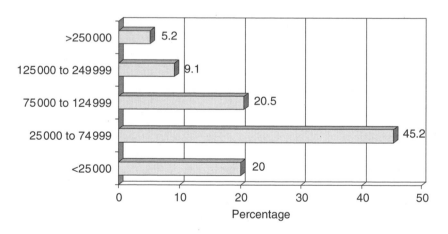

Source: National Survey of Rural Community Colleges (2002).

Figure 4.2   County population

average, graduated during that academic year, and that 82 percent of the graduates in spring 2001 had job offers within six months.

Although most community colleges in rural areas continue to offer traditional classroom instruction, a growing number are offering training

Table 4.1 Characteristics of public US community colleges and their areas of operation

| | Enrollment | | Number | | College finances | | | | | |
| | Distribution | | | | | Distribution of revenue | | | | |
Area Type	Enrollment	Institutions	Enrollment	Institutions	Revenue per student	State	Local	Tuition	Federal	Other
1 Large City	22.1%	9.4%	18 015	112	$2479	43.2%	17.4%	19.1%	13.5%	6.8%
2 Large City Fringe	28.4%	17.4%	12 544	275	$2499	39.0%	20.1%	21.4%	9.5%	10.1%
3 Mid-size City	26.6%	23.2%	8830	207	$2802	45.4%	11.3%	21.8%	12.0%	9.6%
4 Mid-size City Fringe	5.0%	7.4%	5155	88	$2539	49.9%	9.3%	20.1%	11.8%	8.8%
5 Large Town	3.0%	4.7%	4959	56	$3615	45.9%	10.3%	18.0%	13.8%	12.0%
6 Small Town	11.5%	30.3%	2926	360	$3178	48.2%	8.3%	17.7%	14.6%	11.1%
7 Rural	3.3%	7.5%	3337	89	$3457	44.5%	11.2%	21.4%	12.2%	10.8%
8 Not Assigned				3						
	99.9%	100.0%		1190						

Source: Westat (2005), *The 21st Century Community College: A Strategic Guide for Maximizing Labor Market Responsiveness*, Rockville, MD.

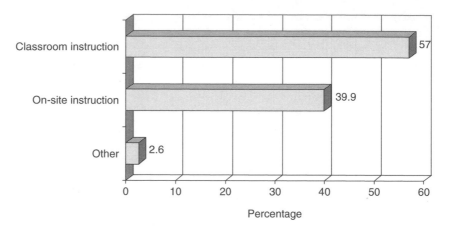

Source: National Survey of Rural Community Colleges (2002).

Figure 4.3   Current mix of on-site and traditional classroom instruction

programs on the premises of the workplace. Among the community colleges surveyed, 57 percent of the instruction is traditional classroom instruction, 40 percent is on-site (workplace) and 3 percent is 'other'. About 60 percent of the colleges thought this mix has remained about the same in the last two years. One-third of the colleges, however, have increased their use of on-site instruction, while only 10 percent have increased their use of traditional classroom instruction. So, it appears that most of the instruction continues to be with the 'transfer function', but the trend is toward more contract training.

About one-third (31 percent) of community colleges reported that liberal arts and college transfer programs had the highest student enrollment, while health care, computer and business programs were also common responses (Figure 4.3).

TRAINING NEEDS OF REGIONS

Most rural community colleges conduct a systematic assessment of the training needs of residents and businesses in their region. Fifty-seven percent of the community colleges assess the training needs of residents, but most do not do it on a regular basis. Among those institutions that systematically assess training needs of residents, 29 percent do it on an annual basis and 16 percent do it biannually. The rest do it in a non-systematic way.

How do community colleges assess the training needs of their residents? They are most likely to use surveys or focus groups.

The vast majority of community colleges report they systematically assess the training needs of businesses in their region. Approximately 82 percent conduct a systematic assessment of business needs in their region. One-third of the community colleges conduct these assessments on an annual basis and 14 percent do it on a biannual basis. Similarly, community colleges are likely to use surveys (84 percent) and focus groups (76 percent) when they conduct their assessments. Many community colleges, however, rely on advisory committees (about 10 percent) to provide input on business training needs in their region. Overall, the evidence suggests that community colleges use a variety of mechanisms to assess the demand for their programs. They do, however, tend to rely most heavily on the largest firms due to their sizeable influence on programming in their region.

Apprenticeships

Apprenticeship programs are growing in popularity. They offer hands-on experience and training, and serve the needs of regional businesses. Promoters of apprenticeships contend that they provide a tighter linkage between training and labor market needs. These programs also offer an opportunity to establish more systematic linkages between regional training institutions and employers. Usually, apprentices receive formal training while working to gain additional experience in the workplace. I was interested in how frequently these types of arrangements were established in rural areas. In many urban settings, unions play a critical role in sponsoring and establishing apprenticeships. Because firms in rural areas are less likely to be unionized, I would expect there to be far fewer opportunities for apprenticeships.

About one-half (54 percent) of the community colleges offered apprenticeship programs during the 2000–1 academic year. The number of students participating in the apprenticeship programs averages 180 students, with most schools having programs with less than 100 students. Approximately 30 businesses, on average, participated in apprenticeship programs. Again, most programs involve a relatively small number of businesses (less than 20).

Faculty size and nonmetropolitan location influenced community college involvement with apprenticeship programs. Community colleges in nonmetropolitan counties had less than one-half the number of faculty (full- and part-time) than those in metropolitan counties, and were less likely to offer apprenticeship programs. About one-half (48 percent) of community colleges in rural counties offered apprenticeship programs, while three-fourths of community colleges in urban counties offered them.

These figures are discouraging. Apprenticeships provide students with real world work experience and an opportunity to learn more about job opportunities in the region. The analysis of the employer data revealed that firm size was strongly related to employers' likelihood to be offering apprenticeships, largely because they have more opportunities, needs and resources. Service establishments were also more likely to be engaged in apprenticeships. As we will see later in the case studies, apprenticeships are difficult to manage in rural settings because the demand is relatively small and the institutions lack resources to develop the programs. Besides the obstacles of scale, distance can also be a problem in rural areas that are sparsely populated.

Business Services and Customized Training

Another area of growth for community colleges is business services. About one-half (51 percent) of the community colleges reported that their campus delivered a business service project during the 2000–1 academic year. Among these services are strategic planning, assessment of worker skills, soft-skills training, and leadership training. Most of these business services tend to be fairly small in terms of cost. Almost 90 percent of the programs cost the customers $5000 or less, and only 5 percent cost more than $25 000. Although community colleges offer services to a wide variety of clients, manufacturing firms are much more likely to receive these programs. Approximately 63 percent of the business service programs were for manu-facturing firms, 17 percent for service firms, 13 percent for governments, and 8 percent for others.

Community colleges reported on the customized training programs they provided to regional businesses. Almost all (94 percent) offered customized training programs during the 2000–1 academic year. These programs were designed for training both entry level workers and those existing workers in need of upgrading. As Figure 4.4 demonstrates, customized training appears to serve the needs of entry level workers more than existing workers. On average, community colleges delivered 85 customized training programs to businesses for upgrading or retaining existing workers. These programs were widely distributed – with an average of 54 different firms contracting for customized courses and accounting for more than 2000 workers (Figures 4.5 and 4.6).

Customized courses are frequently developed cooperatively between employers and the campus (Figure 4.7). The curriculum for customized courses is seldom (8 percent) designed solely by employers. About one-third of the courses, however, are designed solely by the community college.

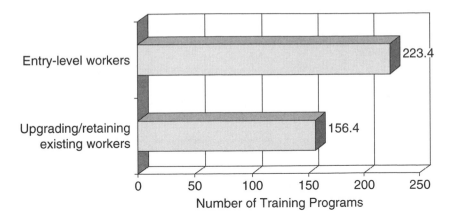

Source: National Survey of Rural Community Colleges (2002).

Figure 4.4   Custom training programs to employees ·

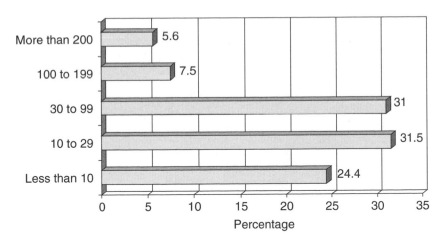

Source: National Survey of Rural Community Colleges (2002).

Figure 4.5   Firms contracted for customized courses

How do community colleges prefer to deliver training in their region? In almost half (47 percent) of the cases, employers preferred on-site training by non-employees, such as community college or private trainers (Figure 4.8). Most firms do not have personnel who can devote time to

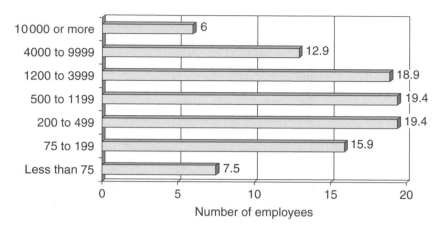

Source: National Survey of Rural Community Colleges (2002).

Figure 4.6   Employees trained in customized courses

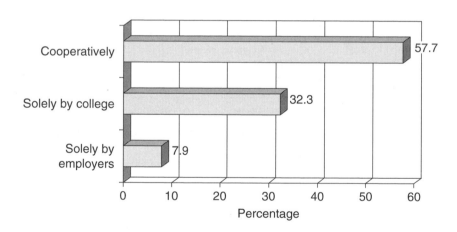

Source: National Survey of Rural Community Colleges (2002).

Figure 4.7   Customized course curriculum development

these efforts, which is why they prefer non-employees to conduct the programs. About one-fourth of the respondents indicated that the preferred
delivery method is on-site by the employer (on-the-job training) or off-site
by non-employees, such as certification programs or at community colleges.

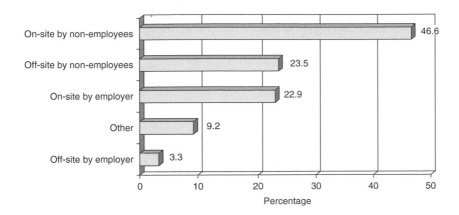

Source: National Survey of Rural Community Colleges (2002).

Figure 4.8   Preferred delivery format for training

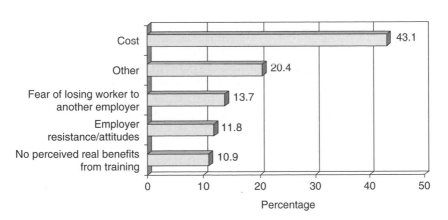

Source: National Survey of Rural Community Colleges (2002).

Figure 4.9   Most important constraint to employer-provided training

The shift to on-site instruction appears to be a response to the perceived preferences of regional businesses.

What are the most important constraints facing employers in training workers in the region (Figure 4.9)? Community colleges reported that cost was the most important constraint. Forty-three percent of the community colleges thought this was the most important constraint. This finding is a bit inconsistent with much of the literature that suggests that the risk of losing trained workers is the primary obstacle here. The employer survey and the case studies tend to confirm the response by community college officials, however. Cost considerations seem to override almost all other considerations. The next reason in importance (at 14 percent) was the fear of losing the worker, and their investment, to another employer.

COLLABORATION WITH COMMUNITY-BASED ORGANIZATIONS AND CONSORTIUMS

Community colleges can potentially play an important role in rural economic development because of their linkages with a variety of regional organizations and institutions (MDC 1998). In this and the following sections I explore the relationships that community colleges have with community-based organizations and employer consortia and evaluate the effects of these relationships on the types of programs and services they offer.

Almost 85 percent of the community colleges report that they have collaborated with a CBO in the past three years to deliver a training program. Who initiated these collaborations? Community colleges initiated the collaboration in most instances (69 percent of the cases), but CBOs were likely to initiate the relationship in more than half the cases (53 percent) (Figure 4.10). (Note that we allowed respondents to provide more than one response here.) It appears that collaborations are much less likely to be initiated by local employers or local government (less than one-fourth of the cases, each).

What are the chief advantages of collaboration with community-based organizations (Figure 4.11)? The most frequent (more than 50 percent) reported advantages are the ties and connections with workers and employers in the region. A significant number (42 percent) of the colleges report that the chief advantage is expertise and experience gained through the relationships. About one-third report that the advantages are primarily cost or access to equipment and/or space. The most commonly offered programs delivered through collaboration with community-based organizations were general work skills (32 percent) and computer programs (20 percent) (Figure 4.12). Thus, it appears that collaboration with community-based organizations broadens the training programs being offered.

About three-fourths of the community colleges have worked with consortiums of employers over three years. Community colleges often (59 percent) initiate consortiums of employers (Figure 4.13). Local employers initiated consortiums 37 percent of the time, while local governments initiated fewer (19 percent) consortiums. (Note that we allowed respondents

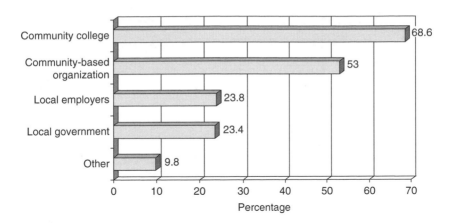

Source: National Survey of Rural Community Colleges (2002).

Figure 4.10 Initiation of collaboration with community-based organizations

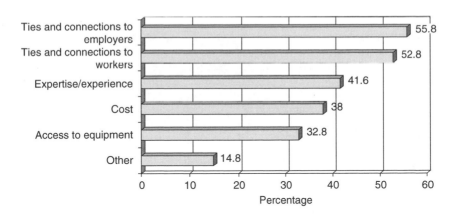

Source: National Survey of Rural Community Colleges (2002).

Figure 4.11 Chief advantage of collaboration with community-based organizations

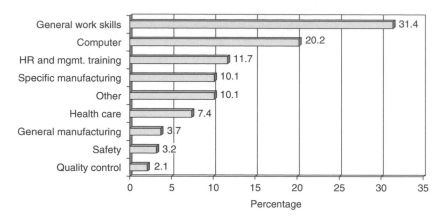

Source: National Survey of Rural Community Colleges (2002).

Figure 4.12 Most commonly offered programs delivered with community-based organizations

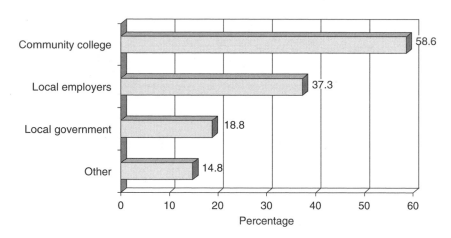

Source: National Survey of Rural Community Colleges (2002).

Figure 4.13 Initiation of consortium of employers

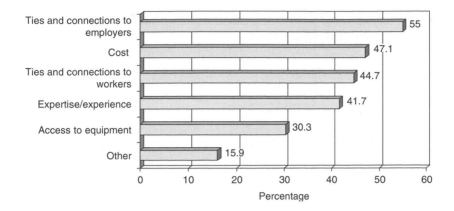

Source: National Survey of Rural Community Colleges (2002).

Figure 4.14   Chief advantage of consortiums

to provide more than one response here.) One of the continuing issues for providing contract training is that community colleges are most likely to provide programs to large employers. The General Accountability Office (2004) found that contract training was offered to small businesses (100 or fewer employees) about one-fourth of the time. Large firms are more likely to have the resources to provide this training and to have the ties with the community colleges to initiate these programs.

A majority of community colleges (55 percent) reported that creating ties and connections to other employers was the chief advantage gained by partnering with consortiums (Figure 4.14). Other advantages such as cost, connections with workers, and gaining expertise were reported. Manufacturing and general work skill programs (each above 20 percent) were the most commonly offered programs to the consortiums (Figure 4.15).

Community colleges that average more classroom versus on-site instruction were less likely to have worked with consortiums. Also, of the community colleges that assess the training needs of businesses, 78 percent worked with consortiums, while about one-half (55 percent) of community colleges worked with consortiums that did not assess training needs. Thus, it appears that community colleges move out of the classroom as they become involved with employer consortiums.

Overall, the evidence presented here suggests that community colleges reap different benefits in their associations with employer consortiums than they do with community-based organizations. Collaboration with community-based organizations provides greater access to workers, while

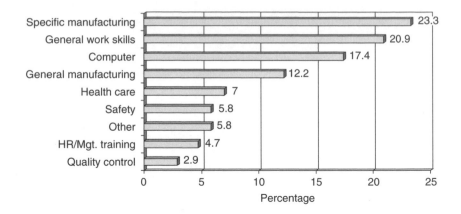

Source: National Survey of Rural Community Colleges (2002).

Figure 4.15   Most commonly offered programs to groups or consortiums

collaborations with groups of employers tend to provide more economic benefits. Also, collaboration with community-based organizations tends to broaden the type of training provided.

Community colleges are deeply involved with these other organizations in their region (Rubin and Autry 1998). They tend to work most closely with economic development organizations (65 percent) and chambers of commerce (68 percent), and less frequently with service clubs (30 percent) and state agencies (28 percent). What does this collaboration achieve? In many cases, community colleges work closely with economic development organizations to put together packages for firms considering moving to the region. Community colleges may be asked to develop training programs and services for the firm because the labor force in the region may not have the necessary skills.

EMPHASIZING THE 'COMMUNITY' IN COMMUNITY COLLEGE

Community colleges have historically struggled over their appropriate mission. Is the mission to prepare their students for four-year colleges or is it vocational training for local businesses? These issues have come to the fore in recent years, especially for community colleges in rural areas. There are several reasons for this increased debate over the role of community colleges. Fiscal pressures have forced many community colleges to seek new sources of revenue, such as customized training. Increased interest in accountability have also pushed community colleges to demonstrate that they are engaged in providing services and customized training for businesses (Rosenfeld 2001).

Most community colleges in rural areas are balancing a broad range of activities. Not only are they involved in basic education and training, they have become critical service providers and are directly engaged in rural economic development. Providing business service projects has also expanded the conventional mission of community colleges of teaching and instruction on campus, to undertaking instruction and training projects outside their walls as well. Customized training programs can be offered at the community college or any number of facilities that are convenient for the employer. It is also evident that community colleges have expanded their modes of instruction to include not only traditional classroom instruction, but on-site instruction, distance learning, and online courses.

Community colleges often carry out their mission through collaborative efforts with a wide variety of community-based organizations. These linkages are especially important in helping them make connections to businesses and workers. Although collaborative efforts have a variety of advantages, they do not necessarily address the most important constraint to employer training – cost – identified by community colleges. They do have the advantage of broadening the training effort and providing more general skills when they become engaged with CBOs. In this analysis, I compared the programming efforts of community colleges that collaborated with consortiums and community-based organizations to those community colleges that did not. There were significant differences in the types of programming offered. I believe this is largely due to the tendency for community colleges to be overly responsive to individual business needs unless they become involved in these types of regional collaborations.

To reach their potential, rural community colleges need to develop collaborative ties with a wide range of community-based organizations and employers. The tendency in many cases is to offer some programs and work with those organizations and firms that respond. This means that the community colleges may not be making contacts with employers in the region who could most benefit from these relationships. Participation in broad workforce development networks helps broaden the contacts and exposure to the breadth of needs in the regional economy.

In the end, community colleges can make broader contributions to regional economic growth and development through their participation in workforce development networks. These relationships help them fulfill their public mission and provide stronger linkages with workers in the region.

NOTE

1. All data from this survey are based on the campus located nearest the business that pro-
    vided the information. In many cases, community colleges have multiple branches and this
    information refers to the single branch, rather than the entire institution.

5. Workforce development networks: the visible hand at work

with Valeria Galetto

Workforce development is a misunderstood concept that is often considered just job training. Harrison and Weiss (1998: 5) define workforce development as the 'constellation of activities from orientation to the work world, recruiting, placement, and mentoring to follow-up counseling and crisis intervention.' Training is only a part of the process. One of the innovations with workforce development networks has been to provide workers with a broad set of services that reflect different needs and changes that take place over one's career.

Workforce development activities are frequently provided through inter-organizational networks that collaborate across a region. In this chapter I examine how workforce development networks are organized in rural areas. Almost all of the research on this topic has focused on urban areas where a multitude of actors and organizations can be found involved in workforce development. Rural areas present some unique obstacles to overcome in the creation and maintenance of workforce development networks. I am especially interested in assessing how the organizational structure of networks influences employer participation and the types of programs and services offered. I analyze whether these networks can successfully overcome the obstacles to employer-provided job training. Finally, I examine the factors influencing employer participation in collaborative efforts with community-based organizations to provide a variety of services.

The case studies in this chapter were selected through information provided by employers interviewed in the survey. In each case study we conducted intensive interviews with various actors of the network, including businesses, workers, training institutions, community-based organizations, public agencies and other partners. See Appendix 3 for a sample of the questions asked in the case studies. The purpose of these interviews was to understand how these networks were established and maintained, and whether they provided advantages that were not available to individual organizations and institutions. In the case of Rural Opportunities Incorporated (ROI), the interviews with workers and students were conducted in Spanish and translated into English. In addition to the interviews, we obtained relevant documents, including meeting minutes, financial records, promotional material, training material, etc.

Few workforce development networks in rural areas were actually 'community-based.' Almost all were regional in their focus. Thus, these networks are not only collaborating across different sectors of the labor market (employers, trainers, community-based organizations), but also across multiple communities. In selecting the case studies, I identified different types of networks, especially in the type and range of services and programs that are provided. I do not make any claims that the three case studies discussed in this chapter are representative of all the workforce development networks in rural America. They do provide, I think, some common ways of organizing workforce development efforts. In addition to these three cases, I also conducted some other 'shadow' cases to gain some insights into how employers relate to workforce development networks.

Three different organizational structures for workforce development networks in rural areas were identified. In the following section, I describe the basic structure and provide concrete examples of how each of these networks operates (see Table 5.1). Because their context is so important, I provide some detail on the history of the project as well as the local labor market in which they operate.

RURAL OPPORTUNITIES INCORPORATED

Rural Opportunities Inc. (ROI) was established in 1969 as an umbrella organization to provide housing, health, education, employment and emergency services to migrant and seasonal farm workers in the state of New York. Two different sets of events led to the creation of ROI. During the 1960s the New York State Council of Churches promoted the development of several community-based organizations (CBOs) to assist migrant farm workers and their families by offering emergency services such as food, clothing, transportation and minimum health care. These organizations, however, were loosely connected and coordinated by the Council of Churches (Mitchell 1996). Most of the farm workers in the 1960s were African Americans from Florida. One of the main crops in the region was cherries, which had to be hand picked. The workers faced a variety of problems in these rural areas, especially housing and educational issues.

At about the same time the federal government's Office of Economic Opportunity (OEO) was given the responsibility to fight the war on poverty and, specifically, the war on migrant poverty. This task, according to Stuart Mitchell, ROI's President and CEO, was motivated in great measure by

Table 5.1 Case studies compared

	Rural Opportunities Inc.	Mid-Delta Workforce Alliance	Wisconsin's Plastics Valley Association
Function	Community Development Corporation (CDC) that offers a wide range of programs and services to farm workers, low-income families, and economically depressed communities throughout New York, Pennsylvania, New Jersey, Ohio, Indiana, and Puerto Rico.	Community Based Organization (CBO) that focuses on promoting systematic information sharing and networking across local organizations, rather than providing direct services to them. It serves a three county area located in Mississippi and Arkansas.	Loosely connected network that provides educational and training programs to plastics employers in Wisconsin.
Types of training	It is a direct provider of the National Farm worker Jobs Program.	It focuses on three areas: 1. Current Employees 2. Out-of-School / Out-of-Work 3. Future Employees: School-to-Work Transition. Groundhog Job Shadow Day	MATC Training Program in Plastics. 2 + 2 + 2 in Plastics.
Number of workers trained	In FY 2001/2002 253 people were trained – 92 received and completed 'soft training' and 161 'hard training.'	A program was offered twice, in 1996 and 1998. The first time about 200 people went through the training, while many fewer people participated in the second. The Alliance implemented the Groundhog Job Shadow Day for the first time in 2002. 226 students in Arkansas and 573 in Mississippi shadowed more than 420 workplace hosts. A two-week program, the Sunflower Employability Skills Project, trained 25 people in 2002.	MATC Training Program in Plastics: more than 300 people have participated in it since 2001. 2 + 2 + 2 (Flambeau Inc. and Teel Plastics are the only two companies that have participated in this program. <ul><li>First '2' years: 11</li><li>Second '2' years: 4</li><li>Final '2' years: None</li></ul>

Edward R. Murrow's 1960 film documentary, *Harvest of Shame*, which documented the exploitation and oppression of America's migrant farm workers. Despite the resources and staff committed to this cause, the OEO lacked a coordinated and effective strategy to reach poor migrant and seasonal farm workers. Projects were run by a handful of CBOs that worked independently from each other. This piecemeal and unorganized delivery system, prompted Jack Sable, then the OEO Regional Director, to take the first important step toward establishing an organized structure which might bring coordination, effectiveness and accountability to publicly funded migrant services in the region (Mitchell 1996: 1).

In 1969 the OEO contracted with the New York State Center of Migrant Studies (CMS) at Geneseo University to provide a variety of services to migrant and seasonal farm workers. The Center formed the Bureau of Program Funding (BPF), an umbrella organization comprised of some of the faith-based organizations mentioned above and other community advocacy organizations, farm workers, and representatives of the New York OEO, the CMS, and the fruit and vegetable industry. The BPF administered the federal grant and coordinated the efforts to address migrant and seasonal farm worker needs throughout the state of New York.

In 1971, the BPF became an independent entity from the CMS, changed its name to Program Funding, Inc., and moved its central offices from Geneseo to Rochester, NY – where it has been located ever since. In 1978, Program Funding, Inc. changed its name to Rural New York Farm Worker Opportunities, Inc., which in turn changed to Rural Opportunities, Inc. in 1985 (ROI 1994).

Today, ROI offers a wide range of programs and services to farm workers, low-income families and economically depressed communities throughout New York, Pennsylvania, New Jersey, Ohio, Indiana and Puerto Rico. Although half of the participants agency-wide are not farm workers, ROI has become the biggest nongovernmental organization (NGO) in the US serving migrant and seasonal farm workers.

ROI provides services to two different groups of participants. The largest group is people who seek one-time help. Although service requests vary, most people knock on ROI's door to find food, clothing, shelter and child care. The other group is made up of those who want to achieve a medium- or long-term goal that requires more time, effort and commitment. This activity includes, but is not limited to, buying a house, setting up a small business or climbing the job ladder – generally from a seasonal job to a year-round one, or from a minimum wage job to a better-paid one. The clients in the second group maintain a relatively long-term relationship with the organization.

In 2001, ROI served almost 95 000 individuals. Most of them were Hispanic (88 percent), young (75 percent were between 16 and 44), less educated (61 percent never finished elementary school), and poor (the participants' average annual income upon program enrollment was $5591). The organization's mission is to enlarge people's access to new opportunities. More precisely, its mission statement is the following:

> Rural Opportunities, Inc. creates and provides opportunities for farm workers and other disenfranchised people to confront and overcome barriers that systematically prevent them from gaining access to economic, educational, social and political resources. We advocate to empower and obtain social justice for low-income individuals and families, and to promote responsible development of communities in which they live. We develop and operate projects, with guidance from low-income individuals and communities that create positive change for those we serve. The foundation of our organization's comprehensive delivery system is a diverse, committed and skilled farm worker-governed Board of Directors and Staff.

The organization operates over two hundred projects, distributed in 11 service categories: Adult Training and Employment; Youth Education and Training; Child Development Services; Health and Safety; Emergency and Supportive Services; Economic Development; Housing Services; Property Management; Real Estate Development; Resident Services; and Volunteer Initiatives. In 2001, ROI had over $73 million in assets and more than $31 million in revenues.

How does this large, private, non-profit organization manage to successfully operate hundreds of programs in multiple states of the US and Puerto Rico? Three characteristics of its administrative structure stand out: centralized support services to state and field offices, decentralized delivery of services, and well-functioning intra-institutional decision-making mechanisms.

Centralized Provision of Support Services

ROI is organized around three administrative divisions – finance, human resources and planning and research – responsible for providing services organization-wide. The finance division is in charge of administering the financial resources of the entire organization, including those of its affiliates and subsidiaries. State-level and housing and economic development directors are responsible for grant writing and procuring funds to run the programs and services within a geographically- or thematically-defined area (more on this below). The funds come from federal, state and local governments, as well as from faith-based and private sources. Once obtained, however, they are administered by the corporate finance division. Kevin Rick, ROI Comptroller, points out that the executive directors do not have to spend valuable time dealing with the main administrative tasks involved in running the business (audits, periodic financial reports to the funding sources, payrolls, and so on). 'Our executive directors really don't have to worry about that because their people are getting paid, their bills are getting paid, we are collecting the money, we are giving them the reports, and we are doing the audits. So I think it leaves them the ability to concentrate in the program delivery and the funding of the program delivery.[1] This corporate financial service has an internal administrative cost of about 9 percent of all grants.

The human resources division develops, communicates and implements employment-related rules and regulations, manages employment-related complaints and litigations, and provides training to new employees and staff on human resources issues, throughout the entire organization. In 2002, ROI had about 200 full-time employees and about the same number of part-time employees.

The planning and research division develops and maintains an integrated computer network system, carries out legislative review and research, searches for funding opportunities and assesses their potential for the organization, and prepares required reports for funding agencies. The whole organization performance is greatly facilitated by the computer network, which connects the headquarters, and all state and field offices. In particular, all the information about programs and services delivered by ROI is entered consistently into the system through the use of the same instrument – a database that has been designed to mirror the service philosophy of the organization. Having an integrated network not only facilitates data collection and data reporting to the funding sources, but also is a key mechanism to ensure the coherent delivery of services across states, thus contributing to the strengthening of the organization's identity.

Decentralized Delivery of Services

Each division director is responsible for raising the funds to run the programs and services under their jurisdiction. There are four state level executive directors – one for New York, Pennsylvania, New Jersey and Ohio. There also is one executive director for housing and economic development. The scope of this division crosscuts the entire organization.

State level executive directors have complete autonomy to decide the type of programs and services they will offer within their states. Consequently, not all programs and services are provided agency-wide. The programs each division offers depends on the availability of funds, the socioeconomic characteristics and needs of the population it serves, and the state office's priorities. Thus, New York state division focuses primarily on farm workers – all its programs and services are designed to assist this particular population. The Pennsylvania state division has recently moved from working exclusively with farm workers in rural areas to also attending low-income people in urban areas, particularly welfare recipients. For the same reason, state divisions differ greatly in the number of field offices and employees they have. The biggest state division is New York, which has 25 offices and 114 employees, and the smallest is New Jersey, which has five offices and 20 employees.

Field offices are mainly in contact with their corresponding central state office, with which they interact on an almost daily basis. Field offices manage their own budgets, which vary depending on the number of programs and people served in their geographic area of operations. In some cases field offices are able to raise their own funds, and thus augment the budget assigned to them by the state division. This happens when field offices apply for funds that are locally granted or when they engage in partnerships with other local agencies that give them access to an additional pool of resources.

This internal set-up results in a delivery of services that is greatly decentralized. Programs and services, however, are offered within a common intra- and inter-state institutional framework as a way to ensure that everyone is rowing in the same direction. This institutionally bounded autonomy is generated through two main mechanisms: regular corporate board of directors and field office level meetings, and regular channels of vertical and horizontal communication at the senior level.

Intra-institutional Decision-making Mechanisms

The board of directors is comprised of 20 representatives from Program Area Advisory Committees (PAAC), two representatives from Migrant Head Start Advisory Councils, 10 representatives from ROI Affiliate and subsidiary corporations, and eight representatives from collaborative organizations. Corporate by-laws require that farm workers retain majority control of the 40-member board of directors.

Almost all farm workers who are members of the board of directors come from PAACs. These committees operate at the field-office level. They are set up following the same structure as the corporate board of directors. The majority of their members are farm workers, while the rest are representatives of collaborative local agencies and the community in general. Stuart Mitchell claims that the wide array of views, interests, and concerns that each member brings to the board, has been one of the major reasons why ROI has been able to remain in business during 33 years. '[This happened] because of the broad diversity of the board of directors and the commitment to recognizing that farm workers can in fact govern and run a multi-million dollar organization and provide the leadership and direction that it needs to help it grow'.[2]

Board of directors meetings are held quarterly. The venue for the meetings rotates among several locations situated within the geographical region covered by ROI – as a way to accommodate the travel needs of the members. They last between one and-a-half and two days. PAACs meetings are usually held bi-monthly. In both cases, staff members attend the meetings and fully participate in them, but they do not vote.

The other mechanism facilitating corporate coherence in this rather decentralized corporation is the existence of regular channels of vertical and horizontal communication at the senior level. These include routine executive staff meetings and conference calls (among division directors); routine senior management staff meetings (among management staff and/or division directors); periodic reporting to the board of directors (division directors and senior management staff) and periodic reporting to the president and CEO (division directors). All these instances are used for reporting, developing new ideas, sharing information, solving problems and planning forward.

The centralized provision of key support services, the decentralization of service delivery, and the existence of well-functioning intra-institutional decision-making mechanisms are the main elements of ROI's organizational structure that account for its capacity to successfully manage more than two hundred programs and services around the US and Puerto Rico. In the next section, I review some of ROI's major training programs.

Job Training and Employment: the National Farm Worker Jobs Program

During the Program Year (PY) 2001/2002, adult training and employment programs received funding from seven different agencies, while youth education and training programs received support from four.[3] The Department of Labor (DOL) was the main funding agency. It provided almost $3 400 000, which financed 84 percent of the adult programs, and 77 percent of the youth programs. In what follows I examine in detail how ROI operates the National Farm Worker Jobs Program (NFJP) – by very far, its most important training program.

The NFJP is currently regulated by section 167 of the Workforce Investment Act (WIA) of 1998 and is administered by the US Department of Labor. Its purpose is to address chronic unemployment and underemployment among migrant and seasonal farm workers by offering 'assistance that strengthens the ability of farm workers and their families to achieve economic self-sufficiency' (US Department of Labor 2002). It stipulates two main activities. First, it provides supportive services to farm workers and their families working in agriculture. Second, it assists farm workers and their families in acquiring new job skills that 'permit them to progress to other employment outside of farm work or to upgrade employment within agriculture' (US Department of Labor 2002). In order to accomplish this, job training and education are offered. Farm workers access these services through the local one-stop centers and through NFJP grantee partners like ROI.

How does ROI operate this program? The first step is to determine whether or not a person is eligible for the program. The NFJP establishes that a person is eligible if he: (a) has been a migrant or seasonal farm worker whose family was disadvantaged during any consecutive 12-month period within the 24-month period immediately preceding the date of application of enrollment; (b) is a citizen or national of the United States, a lawfully admitted permanent resident alien, or a resident under other legal immigrant status authorized to work; (c) has submitted the application mandated by Section 3 of the Military Selective Service Act; or (d) is a dependent of the qualifying farm worker and meets conditions (b) and (c). If the person is not eligible, he is referred to other local agencies whose programs may have other or no eligibility conditions. If a person is eligible, the NFJP establishes that he can receive core, intensive, training, and job-related assistance services.

Job-related assistance services are short-term forms of direct assistance that address an urgent need. At the beginning of every sowing or planting season in the North, thousands of migrants coming from the South arrive in the northern states of the country to work in agriculture. On some occasions they arrive before the beginning of the season. In those situations, farm workers receive food, shelter, medical care or other things they may need to stay in the community until they start to work. After they begin working, they may or may not contact ROI again. These emergency services are also offered to those participants enrolled in NFJP education and job training activities. Jeffrey Lewis, ROI senior vice president of planning and research, stresses that these related assistance services are community stabilizing due to their capacity to effectively retain and provide a stable workforce to the community.[4]

Core services include initial skill assessments, job search, placement assistance and counseling. Intensive services include objective assessment, work experience, adult education and English-as-a-second language classes. The objective assessment is a comprehensive assessment of skills, abilities, and interests through the use of diagnostic tests (math, vocabulary, reading comprehension) and other tools. These tests are conducted at the field offices by a training and employment specialist (T&ES). When the tests and assessments are completed, the T&ES and the participant identify together which of the following training options is best suited for the latter: On-the-job training (OJT), occupational skill training (OST), work experience (WE) or classroom training (CRT).

OJT is a labor arrangement in which a ROI's worker receives an employer's in-house training for a limited period of time. The participant earns a wage during the training period, and after its successful completion he is hired as a full-time employee. In exchange, the employer receives a suitable worker without having to spend time and money in recruiting and screening and is able to provide job-specific training to the participant while recovering up to 50 percent of the participant's wage during the training period. In addition, the T&ES maintains weekly contacts with the employer and the participant to ensure that the needs of both are being met. After the OJT is completed, ROI does periodic follow-ups to verify that the participant remains in the job up to one year.[5] The following interview with a ROI field office employee illustrates how OJTs work on a day-to-day basis.

> For example, [let's say that] an employer called and said 'I have an opening for an operator, it pays $10 an hour. Do you have somebody that we can put into that position?' So, [let's say] I have somebody that wants to work there and . . . [wants] to learn those skills. We can plug in our client in that position with the employer, and we would draw up paperwork, a contract . . . [establishing that the employer] would train this individual to do that job and . . . pay that individual. Upon completion of the training and that [the] individual [has learned] those skills, we reimburse the employer half of his wages for up to 40 hours a week . . . All jobs have different time frames. For example, a packer could take two weeks [to train], while an operator could take four or six weeks . . . Upon completion of that, they continue working there with the employer at the employer's expense.[6]

In PY 2001/2002, some of the most common jobs in the program were packer, deboner, poultry boner, dresser or hanger, and construction worker. The average wage for OJT participants in this year (2002) was $8.48.[7]

Through OST participants obtain skills demanded in the labor market and receive a credential certifying their acquisition. ROI arranges and pays for the vocational training a client wants to receive, and simultaneously looks for openings requiring that training. In most cases ROI tries to arrange in advance with an employer the future hiring of the OST partici-pant. In PY 2001/2002, OST participants were most often trained for jobs as truck drivers, certified nursing assistants and nurse aide positions. OST participants' average wage in this year was $10.46, significantly higher than OJT participants.

WE aims at promoting good work habits and basic work skills at the work-site. It is directed to people who have never worked outside the agri-cultural industry, or to young people who have never worked before in a formal setting. ROI places WE participants in public or private non-profit organizations willing to participate, and pays between four and six weeks of their salaries. Agencies benefit from this arrangement because they receive extra personnel at no cost. In PY 2001/2002 there were very few WE participants financed by NFJP – most were attended by people enrolled in youth programs.

CRT's goal is to enhance participants' academic skills. Participants take classes in English as a second language (ESL), adult basic education, workplace literacy, in subjects required to obtain the GED, and so on. Classes are offered either in-house by ROI, or at external providers' facilities. Participants are placed in a varied range of jobs. The average wage for CRT participants was $8.52 in PY 2001/2002.

From Enrollment to Placement

In PY 2001/2002, 92 people received and completed 'soft training' (objective assessments) and 161 received and completed 'hard training' (OJT, OST, WE and CRT). Of these 253 people, 88 percent were enrolled through NFJP. The other six programs together served only 12 percent. In what follows I focus on training provided within the NFJP.

Several things are worth highlighting regarding training enrollment and job placement. First, agency-wide the NFJP had in PY 2001/2002 a very high rate of success in terms of job placement: 83 percent of those completing hard training within the NFJP were placed.[8] Second, both the rates of training completion, and of job placement over completed training were quite variable across states.[9] Third, we would expect that the high rate of job placement for people completing hard training would constitute a powerful incentive for participants to complete it. The rate of training completion agency-wide, however, was only 56 percent in 2001. Lastly, those who completed hard training had a higher median initial wage than those receiving soft training.

Building Relationships with Local Employers

A key element in ROI's training programs is the relationships it establishes with local employers. There are three main mechanisms that the organization uses to improve employer participation. First, in each field office there is at least one job developer. The function of this person is to reach employers and sell them on ROI job training and employment programs by emphasizing their economic benefits for the employer and their broader social impact for the community. For instance, the New York office approaches employers by means of high-quality written material explaining the variety of important free of charge services ROI offers to them. These services include placement of job orders throughout the four states, services of a training and employment specialist who tailors training to the employer's specific needs, expert referral services for questions about migration and for labor market analysis, and employee monitoring and follow-up for up to one year. Diana Dellinger, a T&ES, describes how she approaches employers in the Albion area.

> Right now, I'm working with a banking company . . . It's in California and they're very big . . . They just opened up new headquarters in Albion, and they're going to have new positions available by next year. So they have this specific training, that may be a month long, to train the employees for the position. And what I did was to schedule a meeting to talk about on the job training [program] . . . Usually people like helping people so . . . they responded very well to the idea. And they will keep me posted; when they come up with the new positions, they will call me or mail me. When they come up with the training type, training schedule, they'll let me know. So . . . we'll have a partnership.[10]

Second, each office maintains a job bank, which is an inventory of all the current job openings in their region. This information is compiled from local newspapers' classified ads, directly from the employers with whom they have ongoing relationships and from the people who participate in any of their many programs. In addition, ROI staff maintains close relationships with other community-based organizations.

Lastly, ROI periodically organizes employer forums. In these events ROI staff informs employers about the organization's programs and their benefits, and discuss with them the trends in their businesses in terms of skill needs and expected types and volumes of openings. Overall, ROI has been relatively successful in obtaining employers' participation. Its bottom line has been to develop strong and permanent partnerships with local employers. As Jeff Lewis puts it:

> The employer understands that they have a partner in the development of these individuals while they're in the workplace . . . It's been successful for us because then the employer says '. . . I'm not in this alone; and I make out better here that I would make out if I would just hire somebody off the street, because I don't get that with them' . . . I think the most important thing is that you're not in it alone. You have a partner. You have somebody who is [as] deeply concerned about that employee working out as you are.[11]

In spite of the apparent advantages, many employers are not interested in participating in ROI programs. Sometimes this is due to the skill requirements the jobs they need to fill have. In others, they just prefer to hire people who have a good command of English or previous experience on the job, characteristics that most ROI participants lack.

Building Relationships with Other Local Institutions

ROI offers education and training to its participants through a wide range of options: on-site training provided by the employer; on-site/off-site (at the employer's site) training and education provided by ROI staff; and on-site/off-site (at ROI offices) training and education provided by training institutions.

ROI works closely with local community colleges and private trainers. ROI participants attend these institutions to learn a trade (welder, carpenter, electrician, and so on), earn a degree (certified nurse assistant, commercial driver), or take classes (adult basic education, ESL, and so on). In general, they are placed in classes that are also open to the community, which helps the organization keep costs down. Because there is a steady demand for training and education throughout the year, field offices are in constant contact with these training institutions.

In addition, ROI works with local Boards of Cooperative Education Services (BOCES) – a county level organization made up of educational institutions that provide services to the community. Some of the classes they offer include adult education, GED and ESL. When ROI sends a participant to take classes at one of the institutions affiliated to BOCES, it pays the full tuition of the corresponding service. Because ROI operates in rural areas, sometimes participants do not have access to a wide variety of education and training provider options. When they do, the decision to use a community college, a private provider or an institution affiliated to BOCES depends not only on costs, quality and availability of services, but also on location, flexibility of schedule, and any other consideration that may be important to the participants.

Several elements make ROI an outstanding training and employment CBO provider. First, the combination of a centralized administrative structure with a decentralized delivery of services has allowed ROI to effectively manage a multimillion dollar, multi-state organization that is able to tailor its programs to local needs. When field offices do not have to seek constantly for new funds and devote long periods to grant writing, or preparing time consuming financial and program reports to funding sources, and dealing with payroll issues and the administration of grants, they are freed to focus on the delivery component of the services and programs they offer.

Second, in ROI decentralization has not resulted in a chaotic offer of an array of unrelated and badly coordinated programs and services at the local level. On the contrary, the local offer of services is coordinated by a common institutional framework, and by a process of cross-organizational learning. Constant communication and collaboration among field offices and between the field office and the central office in each state, has helped

ROI develop a common framework that gives coherence to the practices of the whole organization.

Finally, ROI's staff is convinced that their ability to successfully remain in business after more than 30 years of operation is due to the fact that their organization has been run by farm workers. By stipulating that they have to be a majority on the board of directors, ROI programs and services have been thought of, discussed and approved precisely by those who are its beneficiaries.

MID-DELTA WORKFORCE ALLIANCE

The Mid-Delta Workforce Alliance serves an area comprised of three counties in two southern states: Sunflower and Washington Counties in Mississippi and Chicot County in Arkansas. The organization's office is in Greenville, Mississippi, a town of 46 000 people on the Mississippi River. The Alliance promotes a comprehensive workforce development system, which includes several guiding principles or strategies: working as a convener, facilitator and catalyst; an employer-centered approach; and involvement of a broad cross-section of community leaders. One of the unique aspects of the Alliance's approach to workforce development is that it focuses on several segments of the population, including current employees, future employees and out-of-school and out-of work residents.

The Alliance was created in 1995 when a group of community leaders put together a workforce development proposal and submitted it to the Foundation for the Mid-South, which is a regional development organization serving Arkansas, Louisiana, and Mississippi. The Foundation was created in 1989 by former Mississippi Governor William Winter and former Entergy Corporation's CEO Edwin Lupberger from Louisiana 'to address common challenges and issues that transcend state borders'. Poverty is the region's most enduring and pressing problem. Indeed, these three states rank on the bottom of most measures of quality of life (Foundation for the Mid-South 2001).

The median household income in the three-county area covered by the Alliance ranged from about $22 000 to $25 700 in 2000. About one-fourth of families were under the federal poverty line in 1999, while about half of families with a female householder were considered poor. Educational attainment levels were very low in 2000. In these three counties between 34 and 41 percent of the population 25 years old or older did not graduate from high school. Unemployment rates were higher than the national average. The majority of the three counties' residents were African Americans, varying from 54 to 70 percent of the population.

During its first years of operation, the main difficulty faced by the Mid-Delta Workforce Alliance was to agree on the specific role it would play in workforce development issues. Today, the Alliance conceives of its mission as the identification and mobilization of workforce development resources to promote economic development in the region. The Alliance does not provide direct services to employers, educational and training institutions, human service providers or community-based organizations. Instead, it facilitates the communication among these different sectors of the community, to help them get together to assess the local workforce development needs and to tap into existing resources to address them. Its central goal is to promote systematic information sharing and networking across organizations. Ultimately, it aims at developing the capacity of local organizations to work collaboratively around workforce development issues. In addition, the Alliance generates and leverages resources for workforce development in the three-county area.

The Executive Director of the Alliance is Michael Ward who has worked on rural development issues in the Delta for almost 30 years. The Program Coordinator is Rachel Batts. She is responsible for planning and coordinating specific Alliance initiatives such as job fairs, career fairs and school-to-career activities.

Working Areas and Programs

The Alliance approaches workforce development issues by focusing on three populations: current employees, out-of-school/out-of work people and future employees. When the organization began, most efforts were directed at the needs of the current workforce. Over time, the future workforce began to receive more attention. By 2002 it was by far the organization's most important working area. Ward maintains that this organizational shift has to do with funding availability, task forces' interests, and internal capacity: 'To some degree our interests have followed where the funding is; to some degree our interests have followed where the energies of our task force people are; and we are still a staff of three'.[12] In what follows, I look at the Alliance's main workforce development initiatives.

Training
Currently employed people often need additional skills to either remain in the job or to get a better one. To help them, the Alliance identifies available training programs and works to promote programs that fill gaps in available training services.[13] Community colleges are seen as the primary training providers serving this specific population. Thus, one of the most

important achievements of the Alliance in this area has been the procurement of federal funds for non-credit classes.

An example of the type of training programs the Alliance has promoted is a six-week program in math, English, computer programs, and soft skill training (team work, punctuality, work ethics, and so on). This program was targeted not only to people who were employed but wanted additional training, but also to those who were unemployed. It was a collaborative effort among the Alliance, local businesses and industries, and the Mid-Delta Community College. Participating employers paid for the classes and committed themselves to interview those applicants who completed the training, and to consider them for the openings they might have. Mid-Delta provided the training, while the Alliance took care of the coordination and supervision of the initiative, including the procurement of additional funds to cover its costs. The program was offered twice, in 1996 and 1998. The first time it was a huge success. Approximately 700 people showed up, 400 took a required assessment test, and about 200 went through the training. The second time, however, the program did not work as well as the first. Clarence Thompson, regional manager of the Mississippi Employment Service and an Alliance founding board member directly involved with the program's operations maintains that by the second time it was offered the economic situation in the Delta had worsened considerably – there were a lot of employers who started to close down – which made firms much more reticent to support the initiative.[14]

Another program the Alliance has initiated is the Sunflower County Employability Skills Project. This project established a partnership among the county's Economic Development District, the local educational center, and SuperValue Inc., one of the largest employers in the region. Offered in the summer of 2002, the program had two components: a skill level assessment and a two-week intensive training. This program included basic math and reading, computer-use and soft skills. People who completed the training received a certificate and were given priority in the interviewing process at SuperValue.

In assessing the program, Harry Davis, who is the Director of Human Resources of SuperValue and Vice-Chair of the Alliance Board, comments that out of 25 people who graduated from the training program and were hired by the company, only two left the job six months later. Harris asserts that this is an impressive rate of retention, 'much better than the almost 100 percent [turnover] that we had previously. So, we really improved our retention.[15]

Advocacy

The out-of-school/out-of-work population is made up of those adults who are unemployed or marginally employed. The Alliance's main goal is to integrate them into the labor market. The Alliance contributes to local workforce development partnerships to better serve the needs of this segment of the population, and recently, it has become an advocate for this population. In effect, Ward maintains that:

> We feel that the role we need to be playing, and this is the form the Board framed it, is to be more of an advocate for that population, and to enter the public policy arena. So, one, the programs and services are as good as could be; and, secondly, hopefully they improve their effectiveness and efficiency over time.[16]

In playing this advocacy role, the Alliance works closely with two national networking groups that deal with workforce development policy issues: the Workforce Alliance, a national coalition of local leaders advocating for federal policies that invest in education and training and the National Network of Sector Partners, a coalition of workforce development groups that aim at promoting the use of sector initiatives as a means to enhance employment and economic development opportunities for low-income people. In addition, the Alliance is a partner of the Independent Sector, a network of non-profit organizations that seeks to promote and advance the non-profit and philanthropic sector and to foster private initiatives for the public good.

School-to-work transition

The Alliance aims to link local businesses and industries with schools by developing programs that increase the interaction between employers and students. Ultimately, its goals are to provide students with comprehensive information about employment options in the Delta region, and to develop a flexible and up-to-date curriculum that is responsive to local employment opportunities. In addition, the Alliance is interested in identifying and procuring new resources for schools.

The most visible project that the Alliance has contributed to put forward in this area is the Groundhog Job Shadow Day. Job Shadowing is a national initiative intended to give students an up-close look at the world of work. Beginning with a nationwide kickoff day, and continuing throughout the academic year, students across America 'shadow' workplace mentors as they go through a normal day on the job.[17] In this way, it offers students the opportunity to explore local career options and to employers the opportunity to reach out future employees.

The Alliance implemented the project for the first time in 2002. During that year, 226 students from Chicot and Desha Counties in Arkansas, and 573 students from Washington and Sunflower Counties in Mississippi, shadowed more than 420 workplace hosts. In spite of these impressive results, the organization's target for 2003 was even higher: 1000 or more participating students and 500 or more workplace hosts. Job Shadowing requires a great deal of planning, outreach, and coordination in order to match the students' career interests to the local pool of businesses, industries, and public agencies willing to participate in the program. Thus, the Alliance has played a key role in promoting the program and in getting schools and employers involved.

Likewise, the Alliance has been instrumental in implementing local Community in Schools projects in its service area. Community in Schools (formerly known as Cities in Schools) is a national network organization that helps create and support local projects that seek to 'address the stay-in-school problem within their communities . . . by bringing existing resources, services, parents, and volunteers into a school.[18] As with the Job Shadowing project, the Alliance's role has been to make national resources available at the local level.

County-level Task Forces

The Alliance operates through a decentralized, county-based administrative structure. Each county has a task force composed of representatives of business, industry, education and training institutions, government, human service providers, and other community leaders interested in workforce development issues. Task forces meet once per month and have a two-fold purpose: to build and maintain networks and to share relevant information among its participants.

Besides the monthly meetings, task force members participate in project teams or subcommittees, which focus on specific areas of work such as the school-to-career initiatives, job fairs, and the Groundhog Job Shadow Day. Each county-level task force has a chair (or co-chairs) who represents a community-based entity, and a secretary who is an Alliance staff member. They are in charge of running the monthly meetings, which includes setting up the agenda, mailing the invitations/reminders, conducting the meeting, and so on.

Chicot County Task Force
Chicot County Task Force is chaired by Sharon Cantrell. Cantrell is the Business and Industry Training Coordinator and Adult Education Coordinator of Great Rivers Technical Institute in McGehee, AR. In 2002, she described how the task force works and what it is doing:

> We meet monthly and we discuss things like what's going on in the community, what kinds of activities and events [we] are having at each one of the entities that

we have sitting at the table. But I never thought that's where we actually are doing things. That's more like business meetings in my mind. Because it's kind of formal, people speak freely, we have an agenda, we adjourn, we do all those kind of things. But where we do our work, is in our planning committee, and that meets two [times per month], or whenever we need to. We have met six times in a month trying to write our strategic plan. But it's a subcommittee of our task force Alliance, and that's the people that actually do stuff. We write a strategic plan; we put on the job fairs; we do the groundhog job shadowing event; we are the ones that do the work; we report back to the whole task force: this is what is happening, this is what we are doing. And when people have an interest or an expertise on a particular area that we are doing, they join us in the subcommittee. We have subcommittees that meet not just monthly. This subcommittee may be working on a Job Fair; this [other] subcommittee may be working on a holiday celebration. We have different subcommittees that are constantly working on something.[19]

Besides the Great Rivers Technical Institute, the task force in Chicot County includes all the municipalities of the county, the Chambers of Commerce, the Health and Human Service Departments, the Phoenix Youth Opportunity Movement, the Public School District, and Business and Industry.

Ward states that the Arkansas task force has grown and consolidated faster than its counterparts in Mississippi. In 2002 its two main projects were the writing of a strategic plan for the task force and the development of a training center. Although it was not clear yet whether it would consist of small mini-training sites in each community or a large, single, new facility for the entire county, task force members had already began to talk with Arkansas legislators, to procure their support for the initiative.

Washington County Task Force
The Alliance's Washington County Task Force is also headed by a representative of a local training institution. Marjorie Taylor is the Director of the Greenville Higher Education Center, a brand new, state-of-the-art facility inaugurated in 2001.

Community colleges in Mississippi are the primary state agencies responsible for providing workforce development education and training. State dollars are allocated to Planning and Development Districts based upon the social and economic conditions of the region they serve. Because of the high concentration of economically disadvantaged people in the Delta, Taylor explained that 'we get more money that any other part of the State of Mississippi.[20] In addition to state funds, the Mid-Delta Community College has been receiving federal funds since April 2002, when it became approved as a training provider for non-credit classes through the Workforce Investment Act (WIA). People who are unemployed, or who are employed but make less than $15.33 per hour, can take WIA's non-credit classes for free.

The Alliance was instrumental in assisting the Mid-Delta Community College to become a certified training provider under WIA. At the same time, it is actively involved in the College's workforce development area through its participation in an advisory committee for non-credit programs. The executive director of the Alliance sits on a 16 member advisory committee that meets monthly. Taylor claims that Ward is a critical member of this committee, because:

> He has the chance to let us know some of the needs and wants of the Washington county area . . . Also, he helps us with promoting the classes through his network of people; [and, he] provides us with his mailing database that we can mail out our brochures with our activities.[21]

Ultimately, the director of the Greenville Higher Education Center conceives of her relationship with the Alliance as a strategic partnership: 'they do have a strong network in Washington County and there is no way that we can be successful on our own.[22]

Sunflower County Task Force

Sunflower County Task Force is chaired by Stephen Caruthers. Caruthers, who is the local customer service manager of Entergy, Inc., points out that those who become involved with the Alliance are people who 'want to see economic growth, [who] want to help ensure we become a more desirable place for industries to come in'.[23] Among the people who regularly attend the monthly task force meetings are educators, public officials, and small businesses – with the exception of SuperValue Inc., which is a large employer. Overall, community participation is still something that the group wants to improve.

SuperValue is an active member of Sunflower County Task Force. Davis maintains that the company decided to join the Alliance because it has vested interests in improving the employability skills of the local workforce:

> You really got to be here for a while to really understand the depth of the problem. Being in human resources, I conduct the hiring, [the] training and so on, and try to make sure that we get the best possible people working in the organization . . . I found that many of our candidates did not finish high school; [a] significant number never attained a GED; they did not have the basics in math, in reading, and communications skills required in 2002. So, I had a vested interest in trying to find an organization that promoted economic development and development of people. And I thought that the Workforce Alliance [was] an organization that fit that criteria.[24]

In summary, the Alliance identifies and mobilizes workforce development resources through the establishment of task forces at the county level. We have seen how community leaders get together to discuss workforce development issues, and their rationale for participating in the Alliance's initiatives. Task forces are made up of similar community representatives – people from business and industry, training institutions, school districts, government agencies, and other community-based organizations. However, each group has its own dynamics and priorities, which results in different strategies and levels of effectiveness in addressing their workforce development needs. At the same time, task forces function within a larger organizational structure. In particular, as the next section shows, task forces receive vision, direction and institutional support from the Alliance's board of directors.

A Community-based Board of Directors

The Alliance's board of directors is comprised of 19 members – 12 are elected positions while the rest are appointed. The elected positions, four per county, are filled by people who actively participate in the county-level task forces. The full board meets quarterly, while the nine member executive committee meets in the remaining months, that is, eight times per year. Starting out in January 2003, board meetings are held alternately in the three counties. Board member positions last three years, and one third of the board is elected every year.

Ward characterizes the Alliance's Board as a working board: 'These people come to meetings, serve on committees, manage the organization, and then help move the work forward . . . [This] is a really talented group of people, strategically placed for what we are trying to do: workforce development'.[25] Thus, through their participation in Board committees and meetings, representatives from the county task forces have an institutional setting to define common goals and strategies.

Funding Sources

The Alliance is a relatively small non-profit organization that receives most of its funding from foundations. Its budget for 2002 was about $207 000. The W.K. Kellogg Foundation was its most important donor. Indeed, the Foundation has been supporting the work of the Alliance since 2001, as part of a regional, multi-state project called the Mid South Delta Initiative (MSDI). The purpose of MSDI is 'to strengthen the Delta communities by connecting them with regional economic systems and support structures to create positive social and economic impact, especially for vulnerable populations.[26] In 2000–1, the Alliance received $200 000 from the Mississippi Department of Education. In addition to project grants, the Foundation offers technical assistance and support networks to its grantees.

What do Organizations Get from Participating in the Alliance?

The Alliance does not provide direct services to employers, educational and training institutions, human services providers or other community organizations. Instead, it promotes systematic information sharing and networking across them, with the ultimate goal of developing the institutional capacity of these actors to work collaboratively around common workforce development issues.

The majority, if not all, the organizations participating in the Alliance's county level task forces belong to other community and regional networks. Therefore, there is at least partial overlapping among networks at the local level, what sociologists would refer to as bridging social capital. For instance, as I have already mentioned, the director of the Greenville Higher Education Center is the chair of the Alliance's Washington County Task Force, while the executive director of the Alliance is a member of the center's advisory committee for non-credit programs. Likewise, the Alliance pays annual membership dues to local chambers of commerce and participates in the most active ones. In turn, some members of those chambers are, at the same time, members of the task forces. Thus, given this overlapping between the Alliance and other local networks, is not the Alliance basically duplicating what it is already there in the community? We do not think so. By virtue of participating in the Alliance, members have access to at least the following assets:

1. A forum for problem-solving oriented interaction. The Alliance provides a forum for the sharing of information about workforce development problems, and for the pragmatically oriented discussion of possible collective solutions among interested parties.
2. Coordination capacity. It seems unlikely that training institutions or employers per se will take the lead to design, finance, and manage multi-sector training programs like those put together by the Alliance. On the contrary, collaborative work seems to require an external coordinating entity, capable of giving a unified purpose to a set of interested parties with overlapping but different interests, and to help overcome collective action problems.
3. Economic and non-economic resources. The Alliance identifies and makes available to its members economic and non-economic resources (for instance, leadership and grant-writing workshops) that they would not be able to tap into otherwise. As Marvie Fitts, the Director of Special Programs for Sunflower County Schools and an Alliance board member, succinctly puts it: 'They [the Alliance] afford us these different things that we wouldn't have time to look for.[27]

Taking stock, although task force members belong to other local organizations, their participation in the Alliance gives them access to a set of unique assets, which are indispensable for the provision of collective solutions to regional workforce development problems.

The Mid-Delta Workforce Alliance is one of the few workforce development networks that explicitly made employer needs a central feature of their strategy. By providing a forum that brings together various actors in the region, they encourage a free flow of information across sectors and institutions. The Alliance's structure fits very well into the Workforce Investment Act (WIA) system that was promoted several years after the initiation of the Alliance. A few years ago, the Alliance was approved as a training provider for classes through the WIA. So, in this instance the WIA program took advantage of an already existing partnership that accomplished many of the goals established by the act. The Alliance, however, had already established the networks and relationships that made the WIA an effective policy in this instance. Imposing the WIA structure on regions without these networks is a much more difficult task.

WISCONSIN's PLASTIC VALLEY ASSOCIATION

The plastics industry is a rapidly growing sector within the Wisconsin economy but has largely been ignored by policy-makers, educational institutions and local economic development organizations. In the late 1990s, a group of employers, educators and other interested groups met to develop a strategy for supporting plastics-related industries in Wisconsin, and formed the Wisconsin's Plastic Valley Association (WPVA). The Association has been fairly effective at promoting collaboration among the various organizations and institutions involved in the plastics industry. Its primary objective has been to develop educational and training programs that support the industry. The process has been a very slow one, and there have been numerous bumps along the way. The Association, however, has produced some tangible outcomes and has increased the communication among those interested in the plastics industry in the region. In addition, it has generated increased visibility of the plastics industry.

It is estimated that Wisconsin ranks 12th in the US in the number of business establishments (592 business establishments) and in shipments of miscellaneous plastic products ($6.5 billion). In terms of total employment in plastics products, resin and machinery, among US stages Wisconsin ranks tenth (43 000 jobs) with an annual payroll of $1.1 billion. Wisconsin ranks seventh nationally in shipments of laminated plastic plate and sheet. Approximately one-third of the nation's plastics manufacturing occurs within a 500-mile radius of Wisconsin. Among the factors contributing to the growth of the industry in this region are the skills and experience of the workforce. Wisconsin has historically had a large number of workers in the machine tool industry, and many of these skills are directly transferable to the plastics industry. In addition, the workforce generally has a good work ethic and educational background. Like many other Midwestern states, Wisconsin has lost a considerable number of jobs to global markets and technological change over the past 25 years. Many state policy-makers see the plastics industry as one opportunity to replace many of these jobs that have been lost. Although the wages in the industry are not as good as many of the jobs in the machine tool industry or the other durable manufacturing industries, they are increasing as the skills increase with the technological change in the industry.

History of the WPVA

The initial meeting of the WPVA was held in March 1998. Jim Goldsmith, a local University of Wisconsin-Extension educator in Juneau County, invited several organizations to this meeting in Wisconsin Dells. Among the invitees were seven plastics companies, Wisconsin Department of Commerce, Alliant Energy, American Plastics Council, Madison Area Technical College, Western Wisconsin Technical College, Wisconsin Manufacturing Extension Partnership, Northwest Outreach Manufacturing Corporation, University of Wisconsin-Extension, Wisconsin Department of Workforce Development, Economic Development Organizations (Juneau, Sauk, and Columbia Counties) and Baraboo High Schools.

At the meeting, education quickly became the central focus of the group. The tight labor markets of the 1990s were creating a severe labor shortage in the region and most employers faced a great deal of difficulty in finding qualified workers. In addition to education, participants saw this meeting as an opportunity to improve the understanding of the plastics industry by state government officials and other decision makers. The plastics industry has been viewed as a low-wage, low-skilled industry that offered few opportunities for regional economic development. Participants wished to change this image and demonstrate how the industry had been modernized with new technology and offered opportunities for workers.

Three months after the initial meeting, the co-chairs of the Association, Goldsmith (University of Wisconsin-Extension) and Tom Frank (President of Teel Plastics) developed a strategic plan. The WPVA mission statement was 'to promote the economic and environmental benefits of the Wisconsin plastics industry to the public, key decision-makers and legislators, provide economic enhancement for the industry, and encourage active participation and involvement in issues of importance to the plastics industry.' To move the Association along, the co-chairs appointed three committees to carry out the actions items identified in the initial plan. The education resource committee was established to identify and organize the education and training agenda. The executive steering committee was appointed to provide guidance and final decision making for the Association. Lastly, the implementation committee was created to carry out activities such as job fairs/seminars, educational initiatives, and the Plastics Expo.

An Indiana-based plastics organization, Mid-America Plastics Partners (MAPP), served as a model for articulating their initial goals, activities and mode of operation. MAPP is a not-for-profit trade association founded by a group of plastics processors in 1996. The association provides a comprehensive array of services to firms, including assistance with human resources development, purchasing, sales, quality control, engineering and machine maintenance.

One of the contributing factors to the rise of Wisconsin's Plastic Valley was a series of Economic Summits held by the University of Wisconsin. There was a growing concern with the decline of old industries in the state, and Jay Smith, who was President of the University of Wisconsin Regents, promoted the idea of the summits as a way to demonstrate to legislators how the university could contribute to the changing economy. One of the central ideas emerging from the summits was the idea of economic clusters. The focus of the cluster initiative was to act collectively to promote services and a support structure for key industries in the state. Smith saw three key components to the successful implementation of the cluster approach: educational institutions working with businesses, businesses working together and businesses working with government. The goal was to build all three of these elements into the WPVA.

Probably the most distinctive feature of MAPP is the strong and extensive business network among its members. Participating companies enter into a partnership that 'gives access to current programs and services, but more importantly, opens up avenues for them to identify and take part in the development of new programs that affect their bottom line.[28] MAPP is constituted by plastic processor firms and technical institutions, which pay annual dues to become members. At present, it has more than 150 members – most are firms from the Midwest.

Thus, having this association as an example, WPVA began its work by focusing on basic training programs for the plastics industry, as this was the most immediate need identified by Wisconsin's employers. Madison Area Technical College (MATC) took responsibility for this part of the effort.

Teaching the Basics

The Madison Area Technical College–Portage Campus offered a 20-hour training program for people working in the plastics industry since 2001. It is centered on building and enhancing soft skills. Since the first time it was offered, more than 300 people have gone through it. Program participants held all sorts of positions within the plastics industry – at front desks, production lines, warehouses, research and design departments, and so on.

Large, as well as small, businesses in the area have participated in the program. Andy Ross, an MATC Business and Industry Consultant who has been directly involved with the program, states that 'every plastic producer within the MATC district, at one time or another, had somebody who went through these classes – probably a handful didn't. That's a lot of producers, easily 70 or 80 companies in our immediate area'.[29] The curriculum of the program was developed by Polymer Land, a subsidiary of General Electrics. The company, which is no longer in business, made the curriculum available to any organization, such as an enterprise or a technical school that had the capacity to effectively run the program. The curriculum was offered free of charge. The only requirement was that those who worked with their materials had to attend a four day training session, where they were instructed how to teach the program and furnished with teaching materials.

2+2+2 in Plastics

Probably the most ambitious project of the Wisconsin's Plastics Valley Association has been the development of a 2+2+2 program, which established an educational career path in plastics. The program consists of three levels integrated through the educational system. Each component builds on the previous one, allowing the participant to move from a high school apprenticeship to a bachelor's degree in or related to plastics.

The foundation and first two years of the program is the plastics youth apprenticeship program. Designed for junior and senior high school students, it combines education, technical training and paid work experience. The education and training components require a commitment of two hours a day per week. Four out of the ten hours per week are spent at the plant where the student does his apprenticeship. Todd Spencer, from Flambeau Inc., one of the two companies that have adopted the Apprenticeship Program, asserts that 'the curriculum is very in depth and challenging, including such topics as organizational studies, polymer structures, blueprint reading and quality control'.[30] Students are required to work in the areas of 'quality, machine operations, finishing, materials handling, fixture repair, and set up.[31] The final component of the apprenticeship is work experience. Students have to complete at least 900 hours of paid training, including the training hours they receive during the two years of this program. Upon completion of the apprenticeship, participants receive up to 12 credits of advanced standing from MATC, the next step in the plastics educational career ladder.

In the second two years of the program, students apply their high school credit earned through the youth apprenticeship toward a Technical College Associate Degree. This degree prepares students for more skilled positions within the plastics industry.

In the final two years, students can broaden their background by attending a participating Wisconsin University campus (UW-Stout or UW-Platteville) to pursue a bachelor's degree. One of their options is a bachelor's degree in engineering that focuses on technology related to the plastics industry.

Individuals involved in the design of the 2+2+2 program were relatively (but pleasantly) surprised at the receptiveness of the university system to it. In recent years, there were concerns about students from the technical college system transferring credits to the university system. In this case, however, the university system was very cooperative and that element of the program worked smoothly.

The most difficult piece of the puzzle, however, was the local high schools. The central problem here was that most high schools needed a minimum number of students in these programs to make it worth the investment. There is a startup cost to these programs that is prohibitive for small schools. Goldsmith, the facilitator for the WPVA, estimated that at least ten students are necessary for a high school to be able to support these programs. There is a substantial amount of staff time involved and curricula that need to be developed, and thus high schools cannot support programs that have only a few students. The state of Wisconsin provided a grant to help start this program, but it has proved difficult to maintain it.

Flambeau Inc. and Teel Plastics, both with production plants in Baraboo, Wisconsin are the only two companies of the WPVA that have participated in the 2+2+2 program. In the case of Flambeau, the company offers tuition reimbursement at MATC to those who are interested in pursuing a two-year associate degree. Thus, upon successful completion of the Youth Apprenticeship Program and graduation from high school, participants are eligible for the second two years of the program. Those who are accepted agree to work part-time during the two-year period of studies, and commit to a year of full employment after graduation. Four employees were enrolled in it at the time of this case study. The student's last two years continue along the same lines. Flambeau Inc. offers tuition reimbursement towards a bachelor's degree in exchange for a two-year commitment to full-time employment in the firm after graduation. Because the program was new, at the time of this case study there were still no employees enrolled in its last phase.

Issues

Since the implementation of the 2+2+2 program in plastics, the WPVA has not carried out new projects; it remained basically inactive for a few years and in 2004 has been reinvigorated. The main obstacles that have led to this situation are business competition, employers' training needs, and industry-driven mode of collaboration.

Some of the people actively involved with the WPVA consider that an important outcome of this initiative, albeit difficult to measure, is the unprecedented collaboration among plastics employers in the region. Andy Ross from MATC–Portage, for instance, comments that:

> In Plastics Valley the most unique thing I saw happened at the beginning. When we originally started, several years ago, you could not get very many people in the plastics industry interested; we did manage to get six, eight companies interested but you never got them to host the meetings, they always had to come here, or some neutral [place], you couldn't get in their plants, it was a mindset. Well, as this thing rolled out, of course the group grew, probably more people came from self-defense (I don't know what is going on out there, but I better go and find out) than [from] any, at least initially, real interest. But the group grew, the interest grew, and it kind of took off, and people got really interested and involved.[32]

Employer collaboration was much more limited than the educational partners suggest. Getting employers together to discuss the content of a career path in plastics was feasible because it aimed at solving some of the firms' central problems and did not require contributing strategic resources that competitors could use. It was much more difficult to obtain employer support for projects that involved the sharing of information, resources, and expertise. Flambeau's Director of Human Resources illustrates this point very well.

> It's taught, I believe, to get an industry association to . . . Basically we are sitting at the table with our competitors, so it's hard to sit and share: 'here is what we are doing for training, here is what we are doing for'. . . Well that becomes information that we don't want to share, because we are fighting for the same job. If we find an efficient way of doing something, we want to take advantage of that.[33]

This is not to suggest that ongoing and effective collaboration among employers is not possible. It is clear that the fact of being in the same industry and thus sharing a number of common problems is far from being sufficient. If the WPVA resumes its activities, it will need to come up with creative initiatives that promote strong collaboration among employers by changing the current resistance to work with competitors.

Another issue that may have jeopardized WPVA's continuity is the fact that most of its educational and training initiatives were targeted at providing fairly specific technical skills required in the industry. Indeed, the Youth Apprenticeship and the 2+2+2 programs aimed at building opportunities for advancement that only very few people, from a small group of firms, could seize upon.

Lastly, the WPVA was originally created to serve plastics employers from Juneau, Sauk and Columbia counties. Then it expanded, however, to cover almost the entire state of Wisconsin but the north. Instead of bringing new employers and resources, this rather wide area of service resulted in a loss of energy and focus. In this regard, Spencer comments that 'it was difficult to show value [of the 2+2+2 program] to Fox Valley plastics manufactures when we were talking about creating a program at MATC-Portage . . . [They] want UW-Oshkosh and Fox Valley Tech doing this'.[34] Another important limitation of this industry-based, (almost) statewide organization was the difficulty in getting together on a regular basis. Only large firms could afford to send representatives to all the meetings.

The Future

Although the WPVA is struggling, Goldsmith was optimistic about the future of the organization. Several new initiatives were planned. First, Goldsmith said the Association needs to move beyond education and begin working on new issues. One of the lessons learned from the initial stages of the project is that education and training was not a good 'hook' to bring in employers to the cluster. When approached about the educational and training programs offered through the consortium, many business owners would refer people to their Human Resources Department. Some of the recent discussion by the Association has focused on issues related to technology and marketing. They believe these issues will be much more likely to attract business owners.

Second, the organization needs to be marketed more effectively to other businesses in the region. Several large and medium-size plastics firms have been involved with the WPVA, but at the time of the case study very few small firms had participated. The Association needs to find new ways of providing incentives to small businesses.

This case study also reveals some of the limits of cluster-based development in rural areas. One of the objectives of clusters is to create economies

of scale, which is a major concern in rural areas. Yet, because of the relatively low density of plastics firms in the region the Association defined the
area so broadly that it was difficult to implement on a regional basis.
Although there is a growing number of plastics manufacturers in the state,
they are not concentrated enough in a single region to permit the economies
of scale that are available in many urban clusters.

Another lesson learned from this case study concerns the dominance of
large firms in these clusters and the potential for mistrust among small
firms. Small businesses are frequently concerned that the training programs
are tailored for the needs of the large firms and not for smaller industry.
Similarly, small firms fear they will lose trained workers to the larger firms
in the region. Theoretically, the small firms benefit because they have better
access to trained workers. Yet, they cannot compete with large firms in
terms of the wages and benefits offered to workers. Finally, the cluster must
overcome the resistance to sharing information about production, marketing and training. In some cases, firms were reluctant to have other plastics
firms visit their factory, even though the firm was not technically a competitor.

COMPARING CASES

These three case studies present an interesting set of contrasts. ROI is an
example of a centralized structure for providing workforce development
activities to rural communities. This structure has the advantage of a coordinated and holistic approach to providing services. It was the most comprehensive of the three and addressed a broad set of worker needs (training,
housing, language skills, and so on.). ROI also was extremely successful in
obtaining grants and resources for its programs. The organization was
different from the other two in that it focused primarily on the needs of
migrant and seasonal workers. In the past, there has been a considerable
amount of federal funding for ROI programs. This approach to providing
workforce development services appears to be less successful in encouraging employer participation and in establishing partnerships with other
institutions and organizations involved in workforce development.

The Mid-Delta Workforce Alliance is on the opposite end of the contin-
uum of centralized-decentralized services. Each county in the Alliance has
a task force that identifies workforce development needs. Thus, it tends to
establish deeper relations with other organizations and institutions. The
Alliance can tap into services and programs available throughout the region.
Employer participation in these programs was relatively high, especially
among large employers. This decentralized model, with a community-based

organization at the center of the network, also is more responsive to local training institutions, economic development organizations and other institutions involved in workforce development. This model was quite adaptable to the needs of the Workforce Investment Act programs and the Alliance has been certified as a WIA trainer.

The Wisconsin Plastics Valley Association represents a different model from the other two. This model most closely resembles what is commonly referred to as an industrial cluster, which is now being promoted in several states. Clusters bring together firms that have common needs in terms of training, infrastructure and services. Proponents of clusters argue that there are several advantages to agglomeration. By aggregating several firms with common issues and needs, it is easier to provide services and meet the needs of employers. The WPVA has strong employer support, at least among the large firms involved in the network. It is fairly decentralized across the region, with linkages to a variety of educational institutions and economic development organizations.

The three case studies also vary in the breadth of training offered. WPVA provided the narrowest training among the three. Most of the programs were oriented toward the specific needs of the plastics industry in the region, especially the large firms in the cluster. Both ROI and the Mid-Delta Workforce Alliance offered a broader set of training programs and focused much more on the needs of the poor and unemployed in their region. The Alliance provided much more in terms of pre-employment training and counseling. Given that both the most centralized and decentralized networks offered broader training, it would appear that organizational structure is not strongly related to the breadth of training. There may be other network characteristics that are important here. As I suggested in Chapter 4, the centrality of community colleges or community-based organizations in the network tends to broaden the training effort. Employer participation in the network also appears to influence the training effort. Higher levels of employer participation may narrow the training effort of workforce development networks. The analysis of employers reported in Chapter 3, however, suggests that these obstacles may be overcome through collaborative networks within communities.

The obvious question is: Which structure works best in rural areas? This question is difficult to answer because of the limited number of workforce development networks examined here and the diversity among rural communities. I did spend some time with other workforce development networks, however, and there do appear to be some types that work best in less densely populated areas. The decentralized structure of the Mid-Delta Workforce Alliance has several advantages for operating in rural labor markets. It is flexible enough to address different needs across a region yet it can gain some efficiencies of scale when it is needs to, such as with fundraising. The Alliance also provided the best mix of employer participation and general training programs among the various networks. Although the cluster model has several advantages for rural areas, it is more difficult to build the level of aggregation in rural areas. The centralized model does provide more holistic services but would appear less responsive to regional variability and to employer needs.

What are some of the policy implications of the analysis of these cases? First, efforts to promote workforce development should recognize the role and importance of existing social networks among businesses, training and educational institutions and community-based organizations. These networks are very difficult to establish and maintain. It is also very challenging to promote the trust among the various actors and institutions that is necessary for them to work effectively. In several of the cases, the Workforce Development Act was able to build on these existing institutions and networks, which made their efforts much more effective.

Second, we need to carefully consider the role of public policy in workforce development. There is considerable pressure today for workforce development programs to be more responsive to 'customers', which often means workers and employers. We need to recognize that the two may have quite different needs and it may be difficult to devise a single set of programs that will address both. Employers often want fairly narrow programs that will improve productivity and will often become involved in workforce development networks to reduce risk in these investments. Workers generally need to develop a broader set of skills that will allow them to continue to learn and advance. So, the challenge is to encourage employer participation and help them understand their collective, and long-term, needs which will also benefit the region's workforce.

NOTES

1. Personal interview, Kevin Rick, Rochester, NY, 8 August 2002.
2. Personal interview, Stuart Mitchell, Rochester, NY, 6 August 2002.
3. Adult Training and Employment and Youth Education and Training are two of the 12 service categories in which ROI classifies the services it provides. The former includes five training and educational programs, while the latter includes six. This means that some programs receive funding from more than one agency, and that some agencies fund more than one program.
4. Phone interview, Jeffrey Lewis, 16 October 2002.
5. The Department of Labor requires that each participant in a job training program remains in the job at least six month after the training period.
6. Personal interview, Dunkirk, NY, 7 August 2002.
7. Average wages are own calculations from data provided by ROI.
8. If we look at the seven training programs combined, this rate is even higher, 90 percent.

9. This is true even if we leave Ohio's office out of the analysis because of the very small volume of its training activities.
10. Personal interview, Diana Dellinger, Albion, NY, 9 August 2002.
11. Personal interview, Jeff Lewis, Rochester, NY, 6 August 2002.
12. Personal interview, Mike Ward, Greenville, MS, 20 December 2002.
13. MSDICommunity   Partners.   http://www.msdi.org/community/teams.asp?p=5&s=0 (accessed 11 January 2006).
14. Personal interview, Clarence Thompson, Greenville, MS, 20 December 2002.
15. Personal interview, Harry Davis, Indianola, MS, 18 December 2002.
16. Personal interview, Mike Ward, Greenville, MS, 20 December 2002.
17. Job Shadow, http://www.jobshadow.org/ (accessed 11 January 2006)
18. Communities in Schools, Inc, http://www.cisnet.org/ (accessed 11 January 2006)
19. Personal interview, Sharon Cantrell, McGehee, AR, 19 December 2002.
20. Personal interview, Marjorie Taylor, Greenville, MS, 18 December 2002.
21. Personal interview, Marjorie Taylor, Greenville, MS, 18 December 2002.
22. Personal interview, Marjorie Taylor, Greenville, MS, 18 December 2002.
23. Personal interview, Stephen Caruthers, Indianola, MS, 18 December 2002.
24. Personal interview, Harry Davis, Indianola, MS, 18 December 2002.
25. Personal interview, Mike Ward, Greenville, MS, 20 December 2002.
26. Mid-South Delta Initiative, http://www.msdi.org (accessed 11 January 2006)
27. Personal interview, Marvie Fitts, Greenville, MS, 18 December 2002.
28. Mid-America Plastics Partners, http://www.mappinc.com (accessed 11 January 2006)
29. Personal interview, Andy Ross, Portage, WI, 4 June 2003.
30. Spencer, T. (2000) 'Investing in Our Future', *Plastic Valley News*, **1**(1), 2.
31. Spencer, T. (2000) 'Investing in Our Future', *Plastic Valley News*, **1**(1), 2.
32. Personal interview, Andy Ross, Portage, WI, 4 June 2003.
33. Personal interview, Todd Spencer, Baraboo, WI, 3 July 2003.
34. Personal interview, Todd Spencer, Baraboo, WI, 3 July 2003.

6. Shoot the alligators or drain the swamp: can grassroots efforts make a difference?

Rural communities need to build a competitive labor force, but there are numerous structural and institutional constraints in their way. Globalization and technological change have placed downward pressures on wages and the demand for low-skilled workers in many rural areas. To compete in a global economy, workers need job training. Traditional approaches to job training have been criticized on numerous grounds. Job training is often not strongly linked to local demand. Many federal training programs are not well coordinated and often duplicate one another. These programs also place much of the responsibility and costs for training on individuals. Returns to investments in job training are lower in rural areas than they are in urban areas. As a result, many skilled workers will move to urban settings.

Employer-provided training is one response to these problems. Workers learn best in the workplace (Green 2005). When employers participate in the design of these programs, training is based on existing job opportunities in the region. Employers in rural areas, however, do not invest very much in job training. I have discussed the constraints that employers and training institutions face in delivering employer-provided training. For employers, cost appears to be the overriding consideration. Training institutions in rural areas have a difficult time developing programs because of the low density of demand for specific skills.

New institutional arrangements are needed to address these problems. In particular, training institutions should help to solve the collective action problem of job training. It is in the interests of all employers to have a trained workforce, but it is not in their individual interest to make these investments. Collaborative efforts at job training may provide several advantages. By pooling resources and identifying common training needs, employers are able to overcome the dilemmas of collective action through collaboration.

Industrial clusters have been promoted as a way to promote collaboration. Although industrial clusters are not as common in rural areas, when firms cooperate with others in their industry they tend to provide training to a larger share of their workforce and spend more on formal job training. Collaborative arrangements spread the costs of training over more firms and reduce some of the risk to employers. The primary caution here is that clusters can be difficult to establish in rural areas without a high concentration of firms with similar training needs. Also, large firms may disproportionately benefit from collaborative training programs. Training programs that are applicable across a wide range of industries would seem to have the greatest impact on the local labor market. Such coalitions may encourage broader training programs that are applicable to a wider set of employers in the region.

Rural industrial clusters also present obstacles for training institutions. Because of the density and scale required to make clusters effective, training institutions face many problems. For example, the apprenticeship program in WVPA had limited success in encouraging high schools to participate because of the resources required to develop a curriculum for a relatively small number of students. Distance also makes it more difficult to communicate and to develop a sense of trust among participants. The only way to develop a critical mass of employers with common training needs in rural areas is to expand the region to an area that has no institutional base and employers have no means of communicating with one another. That does not mean there are no success stories of cluster development in rural areas. There are, however, distinct obstacles in building training programs through networks in these settings.

The most important finding here is that it is collaborative training per se does not substantially improve the breadth of training. The composition of the collaborative training efforts matters. Community-based organizations play a critical role in workforce development networks. They have strong connections to workers and employers. Community-based organizations tend to be in a unique position to identify a broader set of skills that are needed in the region and to encourage skill development that enables workers to advance in the region.

These results provide some guidance for economic development practitioners interested in promoting collaborative training programs. Some of the economic development literature suggests that communities should focus more on small businesses (Birch 1987), especially in the service sector. Efforts by practitioners to promote collaborative strategies among employers may be successful in helping these firms invest more in their workforce. Firms that are most likely to participate in these cooperative efforts tend to be the ones that probably need it the least – large firms in the manufacturing sector with a skilled workforce. The challenge for practitioners is to find ways of encouraging other firms to engage in these efforts. Small businesses have fewer financial resources and less time to commit to collaborative projects. Trust needs to be established in these collaboratives so that small businesses will not fear that they will lose their best workers through these networks. The findings also suggest that community-based organizations can play a strategic role in these networks as they maintain strong linkages with employers, workers and other institutions in the region.

I also looked beyond collaborative efforts among employers and examined the organizational structure of workforce development networks. These networks are normally involved in a wider set of activities than just training. Workforce development networks take a variety of forms and there is no single structure that will work in all settings (Harrison and Weiss 1998). They usually involve public sector organizations, employers and training institutions, but there are significant differences in how these elements work together. Some models are much more employer-centered than others. Interviews with the employers, organizations and institutions involved in workforce development networks suggested that these efforts must be employer-led to be effective. Employers are skeptical about public sector initiatives, but they are unlikely to initiate these efforts themselves. In most cases, government agencies, community colleges/state universities or economic development organizations provided the spark to collaborative networks. The trick is to build the capacity of the network to the point that employers will be responsible for developing and implementing their own training programs.

One key to promoting employer participation in workforce development networks is identifying the proper set of incentives. Employers participating in these networks are motivated by self-interest. Appealing to social concerns or community well-being will not likely have much of an impact on them. Public organizations need to be involved in facilitating the efforts, but employers need to take the lead in identifying and implementing training programs if they are to be successful.

Looking at the case studies of workforce development networks, the hub-spoke network of the Mid-Delta Workforce Alliance offers several advantages for rural areas. The decentralized structure is flexible enough to encourage local initiatives, but still offers institutional support and resources at the regional level. This type of structure may be more effective in obtaining employer participation because it works more through local organizations and networks than do the other models. It should be pointed out, however, that the sole-provider model seems to garner outside resources more effectively than the other models.

The composition of workforce development networks shapes the breadth and depth of job training. Data collected from community colleges suggested that when community-based organizations are involved in work-force development networks, the training programs offered are much broader than when community colleges are the central actors in the networks. Why? In an attempt to appear responsive to business needs, many community colleges develop overly narrow training programs that are designed to meet specific training needs of firms. Community-based organizations have a broader set of interests and provide training in basic skills that are transferable across many firms in the region. Community-based organizations also are more likely to provide a wider set of workforce development programs, such as pre-employment training or mentoring. Finally, community-based organizations provide workforce development networks with better access to workers and, in many cases, employers. One of the chief advantages of these organizations is that they have strong ties with local groups and 'local knowledge' that can be quite beneficial in workforce development efforts (Green and Haines 2002).

Community colleges have struggled for decades over their mission. Should they provide basic college courses for transfer to four year colleges or universities or meet the specific training needs of firms in their region? Clearly, the trend in many regions is for community colleges to become much more engaged in customized training. Involvement by community colleges in workforce development networks, thus, tends to solve the collective action problem employers face by providing relatively narrow training. In the long run, however, this strategy is limited because new technologies will rely increasingly on the capacity of workers to learn rather than to develop specific skills. This is a real difficulty for community colleges as they are increasingly challenged to be actively engaged in economic development, which most often means being responsive to the needs of businesses. Yet, the long-term economic development interests of the region may require more broad training that will enable workers to continue learning over their lifetime.

KEYS TO SUCCESS

What factors influence the success of workforce development efforts in rural areas? Employer involvement is essential if the network is to be successful. Manufacturing firms are especially reluctant to become involved in workforce development networks because they believe their training needs are unique. Many small firms do not participate because they fear that the programs are geared to the needs of large firms. These obstacles can be overcome, but employers need to see short-term benefits and to develop trust with the other actors involved in the network. Most employers are not motivated by social or community concerns. In the long-run, employers need to understand how participation in workforce development networks will affect their bottom line. There will always be free-riders in collaborative efforts. Some projects handle this by basing participation on contributions to the program. So, if an employer provides more support, they are able to send more workers to the program. In the end, however, employers need to understand how workforce development networks can improve their retention and recruitment efforts, which will ultimately affect the bottom line.

Collaboration does not just happen; it requires some management. Community-based organizations and other nonprofits can play a critical role in working across different sectors of the community and across the private/public divide. This role has to clearly be a facilitative one. Although collaborative efforts among employers are beneficial, it often takes other actors to initiate and sustain the programs. Collaboration also takes a good bit of time, especially when the effort is trying to build bridges across the private sector, nonprofit organizations and government institutions. Each type of institution has their own culture, language and set of expectations that are difficult to overcome. Employers often have the most difficulty in staying with the process because they expect to see outcomes very quickly. The process needs to establish trust, show some minor successes fairly quickly and recognize that self-interest will still be a major factor in establishing collaboration among the various actors.

Building on existing institutional structures has several advantages. Existing organizations and institutions have networks and capacity that can be used to extend their networks into workforce development networks. The Mid-Delta Workforce Alliance was a master at this. By building an alliance across various networks, they were able to initiate new programs and effectively respond to the needs of the region.

Workforce development networks offer a great deal of promise in helping rural communities build their local labor markets. As I have argued earlier, the Workforce Investment Act has had many beneficial effects on training efforts. I do think, however, it can be more effective by helping build the capacity of community-based organizations and community colleges. Contracting out to private firms to provide workforce development services, which is done in many regions, is not likely to have the same effects as contracting with a community-based organization. Workforce development networks are not a 'magic bullet' that will help overcome all of the obstacles to building local labor markets in rural areas. But they are an important institutional tool for addressing many of the problems in rural economic development today.

FUTURE RESEARCH

Workforce development networks have been widely adopted across the country as a mechanism for improving job preparation, training and counseling for workers without much evidence about their impact. This study suggests that workforce development networks have a measurable impact on the breadth and depth of employer-provided job training. I do find, however, that the composition and structure of these networks matters. Collaboration improves the training effort, but community-based organizations can play an especially important role in preparing workers for work and in broadening the training that employers provide. This research raises several other questions that might be considered in the future.

1. Although workforce development networks may provide incentives to increase the depth and breadth of employer-provided training, it is not clear whether they ultimately affect the brain drain in rural communities. The assumption in many regions is that these networks will stem the out-migration of educated and trained workers from rural to urban areas. If the firms become more productive, wages should increase, which will provide more opportunities for rural workers. As far as I know, there is no empirical evidence that has looked directly at this issue. The issue can be broken down into several questions. First, do firms participating in networks improve their productivity any faster than employers providing training as a single organization? Second, do firms participating in these networks respond to productivity gains through increasing wages and improving benefits? Third, do workers receiving training and support through workforce networks experience more occupational mobility and are they more likely to stay in rural areas?

2. We need a better understanding of how and why workforce development networks emerge. The case studies are based on anecdotal evidence and did not reveal any real patterns. The WPVA program was initiated largely due to the labor shortage during the late 1990s in the region. The Mid-Delta Workforce Alliance was responding to the persistent poverty in the region, but was sparked by the resources available from some foundations. Rural Opportunities Incorporated was driven by the needs of farm workers and the availability of federal grant funds. Clearly, employer awareness and need is a necessary, but not sufficient condition for the rise of these networks.

3. Most workforce development networks are relatively new. Longitudinal data is needed to examine the long-term impact of these institutional arrangements for providing workforce development. These networks require significant investments in time and energy and may be difficult

to maintain. The actors involved in the networks will invariably change. How does this affect the functioning of the networks? Will employers continue to participate if they are not experiencing a skills or labor shortage? It was the case in many of the networks I studied that the employers lost interest as labor market conditions changed or if there was not sufficient progress in the goals that were established. Thus, there may be good reason to be concerned about the long-term viability of maintaining these networks.

4. Based on this study of a relatively small number of workforce development networks, it is difficult to draw any conclusions about which type of network works best. I have attempted to identify some of the strengths and weaknesses of each. Additional research is needed to assess how these different networks structures interact with the regional environment.

A FINAL NOTE

Critics may charge that my optimism about workforce development and emphasis on increasing productivity in rural America is misplaced. Some supply-side critics would argue that I am not addressing the root causes of the problems facing many rural communities. What is needed, they would contend, is more government investment in the infrastructure and especially in rural schools. Although I agree that we are underinvesting in rural education, I do not believe more spending will necessarily address the structural problems in rural labor markets. There is a disincentive for rural communities to tax themselves more because of the brain drain. More federal and state government expenditures are not likely to address these problems either. The migration of educated and trained workers out of rural areas is due more to the structure of labor market opportunities in rural areas.

Others may be more critical of the effort to improve training and productivity in rural areas. Many regions are already suffering from job loss due to globalization and technological change. Improving productivity will ultimately lead to job loss in some sectors. These jobs will be lost to other low-cost regions unless the workers become more productive. There are many benefits to increasing productivity in rural communities. The most immediate ones are the wage and benefit gains. As wages rise, the demand for new and existing services and goods also expands, which generates new jobs and additional income in the region. The alternative is to continue to rely primarily on recruiting low-wage, low-skilled employers to the region.

The most recent economic boom has taught us that there is no necessary relationship between increases in productivity and wages. The evidence suggests that there has been a large increase in productivity since 2001, but wages have stagnated. Why? Many believe the high level of income inequality has prevented the benefits from trickling down. Others have pointed to the immigration rates that have kept a lid on wages because of the increasing supply of cheap labor. These factors, however, apply less to rural areas where the level of inequality is less and the rate of immigration is less. If employers do not improve productivity, it will be nearly impossible to improve wages and benefits. Similarly, if the firms do not improve productivity, they will have a difficult time competing in today's global economy.

There is no doubt that improvements in productivity will mean additional restructuring of rural economies. Many manufacturing, and even some service sector, jobs will be lost in the process. That is not to say that we should not continue to try to create and/or save more manufacturing jobs. It should be recognized that the manufacturing jobs in many rural areas do not have the qualities that make them attractive. They tend to offer low wages, poor benefit packages and few opportunities for mobility. As the economic base of many rural communities, these firms are typically not the source of innovation in the region. By establishing better jobs as the economic base, these firms will be providing dynamism to the region's economy and improving the changes for economic development.

Finally, my more radical critics believe that the capitalist system is at the heart of the problem and the only way to address these problems is to 'drain the swamp.' Capital mobility, technological change and globalization do indeed make it very difficult to overcome the structural problems in rural labor markets. Firms are increasingly mobile and can relocate at sites that have much lower labor costs. Regional efforts to promote workforce development do not challenge these basic structures of labor markets but they can make a difference to low wage workers.

Relying on more federal or state intervention does not seem to be a viable alternative at this particularly juncture in history either. That is not to say that there is no room for policy change to assist rural communities in building in their local labor markets. But the policy-makers need to work more closely with grassroots organizations to effectively bring about structural changes in rural labor markets.

Although I have serious concerns with political and economic changes in the global economy, the pragmatist in me says that these localized efforts are the best way to improve conditions for rural workers until a broader movement can be built. What we need at this time are institutions that link these grassroots programs together. New intermediaries are needed to help build the capacity of workforce development networks across the country. These intermediaries can help support workforce development networks, improve the learning across networks and organize them into a broader movement.

Appendix 1. A national survey of employers in nonmetropolitan areas

I'd like to start by asking you some general questions about your company. All questions refer to this establishment, at this site.

1. First, is this a for-profit or a non-profit company? A non-profit firm is one in which all profits must be reinvested into the organization or in the form of salaries, supplies, and so on.
2. Does this company operate at more than one site?
3. Is this a minority owned company? ('Minority owned company' refers to a company where 50 percent or more of the owners are non-white or Hispanic. A member of the board of directors, and so on does not count.)
4. In what year did this establishment begin operating? ('This establishment' refers to the business operating at this site.)
5. How many employees currently work at this location? Please be sure to include any permanent full-time or part-time and temporary or seasonal employees currently working at this location. ('Seasonal workers' refers to employees hired for anticipated fluctuations, such as a harvest or Christmas sales. 'Temporary workers' refers to employees hired due to an unanticipated demand or to fill in for an existing employee's temporary absence, such as vacation.)
6. Of those employees, how many work full-time permanently? ('Full-time' refers to employees who work 35 or more hours per week and are not temporary employees.)
7. Of those employees, how many work part-time permanently? ('Part-time permanent' refers to employees who work less than 35 hours per week and are not temporary employees.)
8. Of those employees, how many are seasonal workers? ('Seasonal workers' refers to employees hired for anticipated fluctuations, such as a harvest or Christmas sales.)
9. Of those employees, how many are temporary workers? ('Temporary workers' refers to employees hired due to an unanticipated demand or to fill in for an existing employee's temporary absence, such as vacation.)

10. Earlier you told me that you had [refer to question 5] employees. I need to go back and make sure I have the correct number of employees. Of the [refer to question 5] employees, how many are:

   ● Full-time employees?
   ● Part-time employees?
   ● Seasonal workers?
   ● Temporary workers?

11. What percentage of your current employees are covered by a collective bargaining agreement (or belong to a union)? (A collective bargaining agreement is an agreement between labor and management that covers such things as wages, benefits, working hours, and so on.)

12. What percentage of the establishment's workforce, full-time and part-time, is female? (Temporary and seasonal workers are not included.)

13. What percentage of the establishment's workforce, full-time and part-time, is of a minority ethnic or racial background? (Temporary and seasonal workers are not included.)

14. How many of your employees are in jobs that do not require any particular skills, education, previous training, or experience when they are hired?

15. Of these [refer to question 14] employees, how many perform no significant reading, writing or arithmetic on the job?

16. Thinking about all the different types of positions that you have at this location, approximately how many vacancies are you currently trying to fill?

17. Would you say it is very easy, somewhat easy, somewhat difficult, or very difficult to find qualified applicants at the present time?

18. In total, including staff time and all other costs, about how much money has your organization spent on job training in the past two years? (Staff time and all other costs are included.)

19. Within the last two years, how many employees participated in formal training? ('Formal training' refers to instances where workers attend classes or take courses to learn new skills and technologies.)

20. The techniques, skills, and information needed by this organization are changing very rapidly. Do you strongly agree, agree, disagree or strongly disagree?

21. To achieve our goals, it is essential to work cooperatively with other organizations. Do you strongly agree, agree, disagree or strongly disagree?

22. Our relations with other organizations are sometimes marked by conflict. Do you strongly agree, agree, disagree or strongly disagree?

23. This organization concentrates on doing what it does well and takes few risks. Do you strongly agree, agree, disagree or strongly disagree?
24. This organization reacts mostly to outside pressures. Do you strongly agree, agree, disagree or strongly disagree?
25. Making long-range plans for this organization is hindered by the difficulty of predicting future events. Do you strongly agree, agree, disagree or strongly disagree?
26. How much competition would you say your organization faces in its main market or service area? Would you say it faces none, a little, some, or a great deal?
27. How much foreign competition does your organization face? Would you say it faces none, a little, some or a great deal?
28. Does your organization belong to an association of like organizations?
29. Is your organization subject to a periodic review by an outside accreditation or licencing organization? (Accreditation refers to a requirement by a government or professional association that the firm meets certain standards or requirements; that is, the training and skills of the workers meet the standards established by the external organization. For example, the government may require that certain workers receive a certain number of hours of safety training.)
30. In evaluating your organization's performance, to what extent do you pay attention to practices of other organizations like this one? Would you say not at all, some or a great deal?
31. How much are this organization's operations regulated by government agencies? Would you say not at all, some or a great deal?
32. What type of work does this person do? That is, what is his/her position with your firm? (Probe for specific job title; for example, electrical engineer, stock clerk, car salesperson, high school teacher.)
33. What are the most important activities or duties performed by this person in this job? (For example; keep account books, sell cars, run printing press, finish concrete.)
34. If this person performs well, what are the chances that he/she could be promoted? Would you say excellent, good, fair or poor?
35. How long does it typically take someone in this position to be promoted?
36. For the following qualifications please tell me whether it is strongly preferred, somewhat preferred, or not at all preferred for this position.

- First, a high school degree?
- Previous experience in this line of work?
- Previous training or skill certification?

37. Does this position involve speaking directly with customers in person or over the phone on a daily basis?

38. Does this position involve reading or writing reports, memos or lengthy instructions on a daily basis?

   ● doing arithmetic including making change on a daily basis?
   ● using a personal computer on a daily basis?

The next set of questions concerns various aspects of an employee's performance that are used to evaluate a worker's performance. For each of the following please tell me whether it has been a major problem, a minor problem or no problem when evaluating the performance of the person last hired into a position that does not require a college degree.

39. First, in evaluating the performance of this employee, would you say that you have had a major problem, a minor problem or no problem with this worker's work attitude?

40. In evaluating the performance of this employee, would you say that you have had a major problem, a minor problem or no problem with this worker's problem solving skills?

41. In evaluating the performance of this employee, would you say that you have had a major problem, a minor problem or no problem with this worker's non-computer technical skills?

42. In evaluating the performance of this employee, would you say that you have had a major problem, a minor problem or no problem with this worker's computer skills?

43. In evaluating the performance of this employee, would you say that you have had a major problem, a minor problem or no problem with this worker's interpersonal skills?

44. In evaluating the performance of this employee, would you say that you have had a major problem, a minor problem or no problem with this worker's basic math skills?

45. In evaluating the performance of this employee, would you say that you have had a major problem, a minor problem or no problem with this worker's basic reading skills?

46. Apart from on-the-job training, is formal training available to this employee? ('Formal training' refers to instances where workers attend classes or take courses to learn new skills and technologies.)

Next, I will read you a list of ways in which employers sometimes provide formal training to their employees. For each please tell me whether or not you provide training using the particular method. Please remember that these questions refer only to the last position filled which does not require a college degree.

47.   First, does your company normally offer in house (on-site) training that is conducted by its own staff for this position? ('Formal training' refers to instances where workers attend classes or take courses to learn new skills and technologies.)

48.   Do you normally offer in-house training by an educational institution or private training for this position?

49.   Do you normally offer in-house training by a community-based organization for this position? ('Community-based organization' is defined as a non-profit organization that is controlled by local residents, such as a community development corporation, a neighborhood association, and so on.)

50.   Do you normally offer in-house training by a union for this position?

51.   Do you normally offer off-site training (such as at a headquarters or the firm's training center) conducted by company staff for this position?

52.   Do you normally offer off-site training by an educational institution or private trainer for this position?

53.   Do you normally offer off-site training by a community-based organization for this position? ('Community-based organization' is defined as a non-profit organization that is controlled by local residents, such as a community development corporation, a neighborhood association, and so on.)

54.   Do you normally offer off-site training by a union for this position?

55.   Have you provided training in computer skills such as word processing or data management to this person (or the person who previously filled this position) over the past year?

56.   Have you provided any training for interpersonal skills to this person or the person who previously filled this position over the past year?

57.   Have you provided any training on group or team building to this person or the person who previously filled this position over the past year?

58.   Have you provided any training in basic economics to this person or the person who previously filled this position over the past year?

59.   Have you provided any training in basic arithmetic or math to this person or the person who previously filled this position over the past year?

60.   Have you provided any training for improving reading skills to this person or the person who previously filled this position over the past year?

61. Have you provided any other types of training programs?
62. What other types of training have you provided? (Contingent upon a positive response to the preceding question)
63. Has the amount of training for this position increased, decreased, or remained about the same over the past three years?
64. What was the most important reason for this increase? Was it concern about the quality of work, an effort to increase productivity, adoption of new equipment, adoption of new management practices, new employees being less skilled than previous hires, or some other reason?
65. Do you anticipate that the amount of training for this position will increase, decrease or remain about the same over the next three years?
66. Would you pay for additional training for this employee if it was not directly related to their job?
67. Do you work at all with other employers in your industry to identify common skills required for workers in comparable jobs?
68. Do you work at all with other employers in your industry to develop training programs aimed at increasing or improving your workers' skills?
69. Do you work at all with other employers in your community to identify common skills required for workers in comparable jobs?
70. Do you work at all with other employers in your community to develop training programs aimed at increasing or improving your workers' skills?
71. Do you work at all with other employers with whom you purchase or sell good or services to identify common skills for workers in comparable jobs?
72. Do you work at all with other employers with whom you purchase or sell goods or services to develop training programs aimed at increasing or improving your workers' skills?
73. Is your firm currently involved with any programs with local high schools, such as the school-to-work program?
74. Does your firm currently offer any apprenticeship programs?
75. What types of apprenticeship programs does it offer? (Contingent upon a positive response to the preceding question.)
76. Would you say that the techniques, skills, and information needed by this organization are changing very rapidly?
77. Would you say that to achieve your organization's goals, it is essential to work cooperatively with many other organizations?
78. Has your organization worked with any community organizations over the past two years to provide training programs to employers in your area that have common needs? ('Community based organization'

is defined as a non-profit organization that is controlled by local residents, such as a community development corporation, a neighborhood association, and so on. Technical colleges or government programs are not included.)

79. Has your organization worked with any community organizations other than state agencies, temporary agencies or schools, over the past two years to help with recruiting workers?

80. Has your organization worked with any community organizations over the past two years to provide pre-employment training to potential workers?

81. A part of this study is to conduct a survey of community-based organizations that are involved with workforce development. We would appreciate if you could provide the name and address of the community organization with which you have worked most closely with in recruiting, mentoring or training employees. (This includes the organization name, the complete address, contact person, telephone number and email address.)

82. Have you worked with or are you familiar with any other community-based organizations? (Respondent given opportunity to include the organization name, the complete address, contact person, telephone number and email address.)

83. A part of this study is to conduct a survey of training institutions in your region. We would appreciate if you could provide the name and address of the training institution with which you have worked most closely or the institution where most of your employees have been trained. (Interviewer was instructed that if respondent replies, 'haven't used one' or 'I don't know,' to request the name of the training institution 'that you are most familiar with or know about in your area; or, the one that you would most likely use if you needed help in training your employees.') (Additionally the organization name, the complete address, contact person, telephone number and email address were requested.)

84. Have you worked with or are you familiar with any other training institutions? (Respondent given opportunity to include the organization name, the complete address, contact person, telephone number and email address.)

Appendix 2. A national survey of training institutions in nonmetropolitan America

The purpose of this study is to evaluate the current and future training needs of workers in your region in conjunction with the training needs of manufacturing and service firms. As part of this study, we are contacting technical and community colleges around the US. All of the questions here refer to your specific campus or location and the 2000–2001 academic year.

Academic Programs

1. First, please list the names of the five academic programs with the highest student enrollment during the 2000–2001 academic year. Please begin with the program that had the highest student enrollment among the five.

    1._____

    2._____

    3._____

    4._____

    5._____

Faculty and Students

The next set of questions concern the size of the faculty and student enrollment during the 2000 to 2001 academic year. Please remember that all questions refer to your specific campus location.

2. How many full-time faculty worked at this campus? _____

3. How many part-time or temporary faculty worked at this campus?

    _____

4. How many full-time students were enrolled on this campus?

    _____

5. How many part-time students were enrolled on this campus? _____

6. How many students graduated during the 2000–2001 academic year? _____

7. What percentage of those who graduated in Spring *2001* had job offers within six months? _____%?

Training Needs of Region

In this next section, we want to learn more about the ways in which your institution might assess the training needs of residents and businesses in your region.

_____

8. First, do you systematically assess the training needs of residents in your region?

    ❏ Yes
    ❏ No >>> [Skip to Question 13]

9. How often do you conduct assessments of the training needs of *residents* in your region?

    ❏ Annually
    ❏ Bi-annually
    ❏ Periodically
    ❏ Other (please specify): _____

10. Do you use surveys to conduct assessments of the training needs of residents in your region?

    ❏ Yes
    ❏ No

11. Do you use focus groups to conduct assessments of the training needs of residents in your region?

    ❏ Yes
    ❏ No

12. Do you assess the training needs of residents in your region in any other way?

    ❏ Yes (please specify): _____
    ❏ No

13. Next, do you systematically assess the training needs of businesses in your region?

    ❑ Yes
    ❑ No >>> [Skip to Question 18]

14. How often do you conduct assessments of the training needs of businesses in your region?

    ❑ Annually
    ❑ Bi-annually
    ❑ Periodically
    ❑ Other (please specify): _____

15. Do you use surveys to conduct assessments of the training needs of businesses in your region?

    ❑ Yes
    ❑ No

16. Do you use focus groups to conduct assessments of the training needs of businesses in your region?

    ❑ Yes
    ❑ No

17. Do you assess the training needs of businesses in your region in any other way?

    ❑ Yes (please specify): _____
    ❑ No

Apprenticeship Programs

In this next section, we want to learn more about any apprenticeship programs you may offer.

_____

18. Do you offer apprenticeship programs?

    ❑ Yes
    ❑ No >>> [Skip to Question 21]

19. How many students participated in apprenticeship programs during the 2000–2001 academic year? _____

20. How many business were involved in apprenticeship programs during the 2000–2001 academic year? _____

Courses and Services

In this next section we want to learn more about courses and services you may have delivered to businesses.

---

21. The following is a list of courses and services that your campus may have delivered to businesses during the 2000–2001 academic year. For each, please indicate whether or not your campus delivered these services or courses.
     During the 2000–2001 academic year, did your campus deliver . . .?

	Yes	No
Basic work skill courses		
Assessment of worker skills		
Strategic planning		
Other services to businesses in your region (please specify):		
_____		

22. Did your campus deliver any customized training programs to businesses during the 2000–2001 academic year?

     ❑ Yes
     ❑ No >>> [Skip to Question 28]

23. How many customized training programs did your campus deliver to businesses for entry-level positions? _____
24. How many customized training programs did your campus deliver to businesses for upgrading or retraining existing workers? _____
25. How many employers or firms contracted for customized courses? _____

26. How many employees were trained in customized courses? _____
27. During the 2000–2001 academic year, in what percentage of the customized courses was the curriculum developed solely by your campus, solely by employers, and cooperatively by employers and your college?

_____% Solely by college
_____% Solely by employers
_____% Cooperatively by employers and college
100% TOTAL

28. Did your campus deliver any direct business service projects during the 2000–2001 academic year?

    ❏ Yes
    ❏ No >>> [Skip to Question 31]

29. Among all direct business service projects delivered by your campus, during the 2000–2001 academic year, what percentage of the projects cost your customers' companies $5000 or less, between $5001 and $10000, between $10001 and $25000, or more than $25000?

    _____% $5000 or Less
    _____% Between $5001 and $10000
    _____% Between $10001 and $25000
    _____% More than $25000
    100% TOTAL

30. Among the direct business services projects delivered by your campus, during the 2000–2001 academic year, what percentage of your projects were contracted by:

    _____% Manufacturing firms
    _____% Governments
    _____% Service firms
    _____% Other types of firms
    100% TOTAL

31. Have you worked with any groups or consortiums of employers in your region in the past three years to provide training programs or direct services?

    ❏ Yes
    ❏ No >>> [Skip to Question 35]

32. What were the five most commonly offered programs or services to these groups or consortiums of employers? Please begin with the most commonly offered of the five.

    1._____
    2._____
    3._____

4._____
5._____

33. Who initiated these consortiums of employers? (Check all that apply.)

❏ We (the training institution) did
❏ Local employer(s)
❏ Local government
❏ Other (please specify): _____

34. What do you consider to be the chief advantages of these consortiums? (Check all that apply.)

❏ Cost
❏ Expertise/experience
❏ Ties and connections to workers
❏ Ties and connections to employers
❏ Access to equipment or space
❏ Other (please specify): _____

35. Do you plan on initiating any new academic programs or services in the next year or so?

❏ Yes
❏ No >>> [Skip to Question 37]

36. Would you describe the program(s) or service(s) that you plan on initiating in the next year or so? _____

37. What is the preferred delivery format for training among the majority of employers in your area?

❏ On-site by employer (e.g., on-the-job training)
❏ On-site by non-employees (e.g., technical college, private trainer)
❏ Off-site by employer (e.g., at headquarters, the firm's training center)
❏ Off-site by non-employees (e.g., seminar, certification program, technical college)
❏ Other (please specify): _____

38. What is the current mix between on-site versus traditional classroom instruction at your institution?

_____ % On-site instruction (e.g., training on the premises of workplace)
_____ % Traditional classroom instruction
_____ % Other (please specify): _____
100% TOTAL

39. How has the mix of on-site and traditional class instruction changed at your institution in the last two years? (Check only one.)

    ❑ Increased use of on-site instruction
    ❑ Increased use of traditional classroom instruction
    ❑ Remained about the same

40. Which of the following would you consider to be the most important constraint to employer training in your region? (Check only one.)

    ❑ Employer resistance / attitudes
    ❑ Cost
    ❑ No perceived or real benefits to training
    ❑ Fear of losing the worker to another employer, thus losing the investment
    ❑ Other (please specify): _____

Collaboration

In this next section we want to learn more about your collaboration with other organizations.

41. Have you collaborated with community-based organizations in your region over the past three years to deliver training programs?

    ❑ Yes
    ❑ No >>> [Skip to Question 46]

42. Who initiated this collaboration with the community-based organizations? (Check all that apply.)

    ❑ We (the training institution) did
    ❑ The community-based organizations
    ❑ Local employer(s)
    ❑ Local government
    ❑ Other (please specify): _____

43. What do you consider to be the chief advantages of this collaboration with community-based organizations? (Check all that apply.)

    ❑ Cost
    ❑ Expertise/experience
    ❑ Ties and connections to workers
    ❑ Ties and connections to employers

❑ Access to equipment or space
❑ Other (please specify): _____

44. What were the five most commonly offered programs or services you delivered in collaboration with community-based organizations? Please begin with the most commonly offered of the five.

    1. _____

    2. _____

    3. _____

    4. _____

    5. _____

45. A part of this study is to conduct a survey of community-based organizations that are involved with workforce development. We would appreciate if you would provide the name(s) and address(es) of the community organization(s) with which you have worked most closely in recruiting, mentoring, or training employees.

(1) Organization's Name: _____

    Contact Person: _____

    Address: _____

        _____

    Telephone #:   _____

    Email Address: _____

(2) Organization's Name: _____

    Contact Person: _____

    Address: _____

        _____

    Telephone #:   _____

    Email Address: _____

Involvement

The final set of questions concern your campus' involvement in local economic development.

---

46. For each of the following, please indicate on a scale from 1 to 4, where 1 is 'not at all' and 4 is 'a lot', how much your institution participates, serves, or interacts with the following groups in your city or region?

	Not at all	Rarely	Sometimes	A lot
Economic Development Organizations	1	2	3	4
The Chambers of Commerce	1	2	3	4
Workforce Investment Boards	1	2	3	4
Local Government Representatives	1	2	3	4
State Government Representatives	1	2	3	4
Business and Professional Organizations, Labor Unions or Industry Boards	1	2	3	4
Service Clubs (Lions, Rotary Club, etc.)	1	2	3	4

YOUR CONTRIBUTION IS VERY MUCH APPRECIATED!
Please return this completed survey in the business reply envelope provided to:
University of Wisconsin Survey Center
630 W. Mifflin St. Room 174
Madison, WI 53703-2636

Appendix 3.   Questionnaire for case studies (ROI case)

I.   History

1.   Why and how did Rural Opportunities Inc. (ROI) get started?
2.   Who participated in its creation?
3.   Have the headquarters of the organization always been in Rochester?
4.   Were the rest of the offices added gradually (New York, Pennsylvania, New Jersey, Ohio, Indiana, and Puerto Rico)? If so, could you please tell us how that process took place, for instance the years of the new additions, why were they added, etc.?

II.   Organizational Structure

5.   How many full-time and part-time employees work at ROI?
6.   Can you describe the administrative structure of ROI?
7.   What type of relationships do the headquarters and the 46 field offices – located throughout the five states and Puerto Rico – maintain?
8.   Is there a central office in each state that coordinates all the activities that take place in its territory? If not, how are they organized?
9.   Can you describe the relationships among field offices located in the same state, and among offices located in different states?
10.   ROI has at least two affiliated corporations, the Rural Housing Action Corporation, Inc., and the Rural Community Enterprise Center, Inc. When and why were these organizations created? In the day-to-day operations, what does it mean that they are 'affiliated corporations'? What are their relationships with ROI?

III.   Programs and Services

11.   What types of programs and services are currently offered by ROI? Can you please describe them?
12.   How are these programs and services funded?
13.   According to the information posted in the website, not all ROI's programs and services are offered in the five states and Puerto Rico. Why

is this the case? Or, in other words, why are some programs offered in some states and not in others? Does this have to do with local needs, funding, and/or partners willing to work with ROI staff?

14. Do you overlap much with other agencies and organizations?
15. We are particularly interested in workforce development and job training programs in rural areas. Can you please describe in detail these programs? When did they get started? What are their main goals? How many people do they serve per year? How does the organization measure their success? How are they funded?
16. What are the obstacles ROI faces in providing training to migrant workers? How do you try to overcome those obstacles?
17. How specific or general are the training programs? In other words, are they geared for specific firms or general enough to provide workers with several different types of opportunities?

IV. Relationship with Employers

18. Can you please describe ROI's relationships with employers?
19. How do you develop relationships with employers?
20. Do you work with specific employers or groups?
21. What type of employers (size, industry, presence/absence of unions, workforce characteristics, location, etc.) are more likely to collaborate with ROI's workforce development initiatives?
22. What are the main problems and barriers in getting employers to collaborate with ROI's workforce development initiatives?
23. What type of training/services does ROI offer to employers?

V. Relationship with Community Colleges

24. Do you work at all with Community Colleges?
25. Can you please describe ROI's relationship with Community Colleges?
26. In which sense ROI's workforce development and training programs are different from the ones offered by businesses and Community Colleges? In other words, what does ROI offer/do that they don't?
27. Is there much 'overlapping' among businesses, Community Colleges and ROI's programs and services? If that is the case, how are you able to collaborate with each other?

VI. Other Partners

28. Can you please characterize ROI's relationship with its partners?
29. Who approaches whom in a partnership? Are they short- or long-run?

VII. Board of Directors

30.   How often does the Board of Directors meet?
31.   Where do the meetings take place?
32.   Who sets the agenda?
33.   How do Board members get selected?
34.   How long does a Board member's position last?

References

Allen, John C. and Don A. Dillman (1994), *Against All Odds: Rural Community in the Information Age*, Boulder, CO: Westview Press.

Autry, George and Sara Rubin (1998), *Expanding Economic and Educational Opportunity in Distressed Rural Areas: A Conceptual Framework for the Rural Community College Initiative*, Chapel Hill, NC: MDC.

Bartik, Timothy J. (2001), *Jobs for the Poor: Can Labor Demand Policies Help?*, New York: Russell Sage Foundation.

Beaulieu, Lionel J. and David Mulkey (eds) (1995), *Investing in People: The Human Capital Needs of Rural America*, Boulder, CO: Westview Press.

Becker, Gary (1962), 'Investment in human capital: a theoretical analysis', *Journal of Political Economy*, **70** (1), 9–49.

Beggs, John J., Valeria A. Haines and Jeanne S. Hurlbert (1996), 'Revisiting the rural-urban contrast: personal networks in metropolitan and non-metropolitan settings', *Rural Sociology*, **61** (2), 306–25.

Birch, David L. (1987), *Job Creation in America: How Our Smallest Companies Put the Most People to Work*, New York: The Free Press.

Blanchflower, David G. and Andrew J. Oswald (1996), *The Wage Curve*, Cambridge, MA: MIT Press.

Brint, Steven (2003), 'Few remaining dreams: community colleges since 1985', *ANNALS, AAPSS*, **586**, 16–37.

Brown, Charles, James Hamilton and James Medoff (1990), *Employers: Large and Small*, Cambridge, MA: Harvard University Press.

Dougherty, Kevin J. (2003), 'The uneven distribution of employee training by community colleges: description and explanation', *ANNALS, AAPSS*, **586**, 62–91.

Dresser, Laura (2000), *Building Jobs with a Future in Wisconsin: Lessons from Dane County*, Madison, WI: Center on Wisconsin Strategy.

Fitzgerald, Joan (1998), 'Is networking always the answer? Networking among community colleges to increase their capacity in business outreach', *Economic Development Quarterly*, **12** (1), 30–40.

Florida, Richard (2002), *The Rise of the Creative Class: And How It's Transforming Work, Leisure, Community and Everyday Life*, New York: Basic Books.

Foundation for the Mid South (2001), 'We can do better by working together', 2000–2001 report to the region, Jackson, MS.

Frazis, Harley J., Diane E. Herz and Michael W. Horrigan (1995), 'Employer-provided training: results from a new survey', *Monthly Labor Review*, **118**, 3–17.

Frazis, Harley, Maury Gittleman and Mary Joyce (2000), 'Correlates of training: an analysis using both employer and employee characteristics', *Industrial and Labor Relations Review*, **53** (3), 443–62.

Frazis, Harley, Maury Gittleman, Michael Horrigan and Mary Joyce (1998), 'Results from the 1995 survey of employer-provided training', *Monthly Labor Review*, **121**, 3–13.

General Accounting Office (GAO) (2003), *Multiple Employment and Training Programs: Funding and Performance Measures for Major Programs*, GAO-03-589, Washington, DC: GAO.

Gibbs, Robert M., Paul L. Swaim and Ruy Teixeira (1998), *Rural Education and Training in the New Economy: The Myth of the Rural Skills Gap*, Ames, IA: Iowa State University Press.

Gibbs, Robert, Lorin Kusmin and John Cromartie (2004), 'Low-skill jobs: a shrinking share of the rural economy', *Amber Waves*, **2** (5), accessed 26 February, 2006, at www.ers.usda.gov/AmberWaves/AllIssues/ShowIssue. asp?Issue=November 04.

Giloth, Robert (2000), 'Learning from the field: economic growth and workforce development in the 1990s', *Economic Development Quarterly*, **14** (4), 340–59.

Glasmeier, Amy K. and Marie Howland (1995), *From Combines to Computers: Rural Services and Development in the Age of Information Technology*, Albany, NY: State University of New York Press.

Glasmeier, Amy, A. Kays and J. Thompson (1995), *Branch Plants and Rural Development in the Age of Globalization*, Washington, DC: The Aspen Institute, Rural Economic Policy Program.

Granovetter, Mark S. (1995), *Getting a Job: A Study of Contacts and Careers*, 2nd edn, Chicago, IL: University of Chicago Press.

Green, Gary Paul (2005), 'School-to-work programs in rural America', *Journal of Research in Rural Education*, **20** (16), accessed 30 January, 2006 at www.umaine.edu/jrre/20-16.pdf.

Green, Gary Paul and Anna Haines (2002), *Asset Building and Community Development*, Thousand Oaks, CA: Sage Publications.

Green, Gary P., Leann M. Tigges and Daniel Diaz (1999), 'Racial and ethnic differences in job search strategies in Atlanta, Boston, and Los Angeles', *Social Science Quarterly*, **80** (2), 263–78.

Green, Gary Paul, Valeria Galetto and Anna Haines (2003), 'Collaborative job training in rural America', *Journal of Research in Rural Education*, **18** (2), 78–85.

Greenberg, Elizabeth J., Paul L. Swaim and Ruy Teixeira (1995), 'Literacy of the adult rural workforce', in Robert M. Gibbs, Paul L. Swaim and Ruy Teixeira (eds), *Rural Education and Training in the New Economy*, Ames, IA: Iowa State University Press, pp. 81–96.

Harrison, Bennett and Marcus Weiss (1998), *Workforce Development Networks: Community-Based Organizations and Regional Alliances*, Thousand Oaks, CA: Sage Publications.

Holzer, Harry J. (1991), 'The spatial mismatch hypothesis: what has the evidence shown?', *Urban Studies*, **28** (1), 105–22.

Holzer, Harry J. (1996), *What Employers Want: Job Prospects for Less-Educated Workers*, New York: Russell Sage Foundation.

Jensen, Leif, Jill L. Findeis, Wan-Ling Hsu, and Jason P. Schachter (1999), 'Slipping into and out of underemployment: another disadvantage for nonmetropolitan workers', *Rural Sociology*, **64** (3), 417–38.

Kane, Thomas J. and Cecilia Elina Rouse (1999), 'The community college: educating students at the margin between college and work', *Journal of Economic Perspectives*, **13** (1), 63–84.

Kent, Norma (1991), 'Partners for the future: business & community colleges team up', *Community, Technical, and Junior College Journal*, **61** (4), 31–5.

Kirschenman, Joleen and Katherine Neckerman (1991), 'We'd love to hire them but . . .', in Christopher Jencks and Paul Peterson (eds), *The Urban Underclass*, Washington, DC: Brookings Institution, pp. 203–32.

Knoke, David and Arne L. Kalleberg (1994), 'Job training in US organizations', *American Sociological Review*, **59** (4), 537–46.

Krueger, A.B. (1993), 'How computers have changed the wage structure: evidence from microdata, 1984–1989', *Quarterly Journal of Economics*, **108**, 33–60.

Lichter, Daniel T. and Janice A. Costanzo (1987), 'Nonmetropolitan underemployment and labor force composition', *Rural Sociology*, **52** (3), 329–44.

Lynch, Lisa M. and S.E. Black (1998), 'Beyond the incidence of employer provided-training', *Industrial and Labor Relations Review*, **52** (1), 64–81.

Lyson, Thomas A. and Charles M. Tolbert (1996), 'Small manufacturing and nonmetropolitan socioeconomic well-being', *Environment and Planning A*, **28**, 1779–94.

Markusen, Ann (1987), *Regions: The Economics and Politics of Territory*, Totowa, NJ: Rowman and Littlefield.

Marshall, Ray and Marc Tucker (1992), *Thinking for a Living*, New York: Basic Books.

McGranahan, David A. (1988), 'Rural workers in the national economy', in David L. Brown, J. Norman Reid, Herman Bluestone, David A. McGranahan and Sara M. Mazie (eds), *Rural Economic Development in the 1980s: Prospects for the Future*, Washington, DC: US Department of Agriculture, Economic Research Service, pp. 29–48.

McGranahan, David A. and Linda M. Ghelfi (1998), 'Current trends in the supply and demand for education in rural and urban areas', in Robert M. Gibbs, Paul L. Swaim and Ruy Teixeira (eds), *Rural Education and Training in the New Economy: The Myth of the Rural Skills Gap*, Ames, IA: Iowa State University Press, pp. 131–71.

MDC (1998), *Expanding Economic and Educational Opportunity in Distressed Rural Areas: A Conceptual Framework for the Rural Community College Initiative*, Chapel Hill, NC: MDC, Inc.

Melendez, Edwin and Bennett Harrison (1998), 'Matching the disadvantaged to job opportunities: structural explanations for the past successes of the Center for Employment Training', *Economic Development Quarterly*, **12** (1), 3–11.

Mitchell, Stuart J. (1996), 'The history of Rural Opportunities, Inc', unpublished manuscript.

Molina, Feida (1998), *Making Connections: A Study of Employment Linkage Programs*, Washington, DC: Center for Community Change.

Osterman, Paul (2001), 'Employers in the low-wage/low-skill labor market', in Richard Kazis and Marc S. Miller (eds), *Low-Wage Workers in the New Economy*, Washington, DC: The Urban Institute Press, pp. 67–88.

Parker, Eric, and Joel Rogers (1996), 'The Wisconsin Regional Training Partnership: lessons for national policy', National Center for the Workplace working paper no. 3.

Piore, Michael and Charles Sabel (1984), *The Second Industrial Divide*, New York: Basic Books.

Pitcoff, Winton (1998), 'Developing workers: community-based job training brings families out of poverty', *Shelterforce Online*, **102** (November/December), accessed 10 March 2006, on www.nhi.org/online/issues/102/jobs.html.

Porter, Michael E. (2000), 'Location, competition and economic development: local clusters in a global economy', *Economic Development Quarterly*, **14** (1), 15–34.

Rogers, Joel, Wolfgang Streeck, and Eric Parker (1990), 'The Wisconsin training effort', in James Conant, Robert Haveman, and Jack Huddleston (eds), *Dollars and Sense: Public Choices and the Wisconsin Budget*, vol. 2, Madison, WI: LaFollette Institute of Public Affairs, University of Wisconsin.

Romo, Frank P. and Michael Schwartz (1995), 'The structural embedded-ness of business decisions: the migration of manufacturing plants in New York state, 1960 to 1985', *American Sociological Review*, **60** (6), 874–907.

Rosenfeld, Stuart A. (2001), 'Rural community colleges: creating institutional hybrids for the new economy', *Rural America*, **16** (2), 2–8.

Rubin, Sara, and George Autry (1998), 'Rural community colleges: catalysts for economic renewal', *Policy Paper* (September), 1–8, Denver, CO: Education Commission of the States.

Rural Opportunities, Inc. (1994), *25: Celebrating a Silver Anniversary, Anticipating a Golden Future*, Rochester, NY: Rural Opportunities, Inc.

Stanback, Thomas M. Jr. and Thierry J. Noyelle (1982), *Cities in Transition: Changing Job Structure in Atlanta, Denver, Buffalo, Phoenix, Columbus (Ohio), Nashville, Charlotte*, Totowa, NJ: Allanheld, Osmun and Company.

Stern, David, Neal Finkelstein, James R. Stone III, John Latting and Carolyn Dornsife (1994), *Research on School-to-Work Transition Programs in the United States*, Berkeley, CA: National Center for Research in Vocational Education.

Streeck, Wolfgang (1989), 'Skills and the limits of neo-liberalism: the enterprise of the future as a place of learning', *Work, Employment and Society*, **3** (1), 89–104.

Swaim, Paul L. (1995), 'Job training lags for rural workers', *Rural Development Perspectives*, **10** (3), 53–60.

Summers, Gene F., Sharon D. Evans, Frank Clemente, E. M. Beck and Jon Minkoff (1976), *Industrial Invasion of Nonmetropolitan America: A Quarter Century of Experience*, New York: Praeger Publishers.

Teixeira, Ruy and David A. McGranahan (1998), 'Rural employer demand and worker skills', in Robert M. Gibbs, Paul L. Swaim, and Ruy Teixeira (eds), *Rural Education and Training in the New Economy: The Myth of the Rural Skills Gap*, Ames, IA: Iowa State University Press, pp. 115–29.

Tigges, Leann M., and Deborah M. Tootle (1990), 'Labor supply, labor demand, and men's underemployment in rural and urban labor markets', *Rural Sociology*, **55** (3), 328–56.

Tilly, Chris (1996), *Half a Job: Bad and Good Part-Time Jobs in a Changing Labor Market*, Philadelphia, PA: Temple University Press.

Tolbert, Charles M., Thomas A. Lyson and Michael D. Irwin (1998), 'Local capitalism, civic engagement, and socioeconomic well-being', *Social Forces*, **77** (2), 401–27.

US Department of Agriculture (1991), 'Education and rural economic development: strategies for the 1990s', Agriculture and Rural Economy Division, Economic Research Service staff report no. AGES 9153, Washington, DC.

US Department of Education, National Center for Education Statistics (2003), *Public Elementary/Secondary School Universe Survey*, Washington, DC: US Government Printing Office.

US Department of Education, National Center for Education Statistics (2004), *Internet Access in US Public Schools and Classrooms: 1994–2002*, Washington, DC: US Government Printing Office.

US Department of Education, National Center for Education Statistics (2005), *The Condition of Education 2005*, NCES 2005-094, Washington, DC: US Government Printing Office.

US Department of Education, National Center for Education Statistics (2006), 'Schools and staffing survey, 1999–2000', Washington, DC, accessed 2 March, 2006 at www.nces.ed.gov/surveys/SASS/tables.asp.

US Department of Labor, Employment and Training Administration, Division of Seasonal Farmworker Programs, 'The National Farmworker Jobs Program', accessed 16 October 2002 at wdsc.doleta.gov/msfw/html/facts.asp.

US Government Accountability Office (2004), 'Public community colleges and technical schools: most schools use both credit and noncredit programs for workforce development', Washington, DC.

Veum, Jonathan R. (1995), 'Sources of training and their impact on wages', *Industrial and Labor Relations Review*, **48** (4), 812–25.

Westat (2005), *The 21st Century Community College: A Strategic Guide for Maximizing Labor Market Responsiveness*, Rockville, MD: Westat.

Index